TO

_____

FROM

_____

D1056674

BREAKING THE
POWER OF
THE MASK

Discover Healing, Freedom, and Joy on Your
Journey with God

JOCELYN J. JONES

Contents

This book is dedicated to anyone who is suffering in silence behind a mask. I pray you find healing, freedom, and hope on your journey ahead.

Acknowledgments

This book would not have been possible without God. All glory and honor belongs to Him, who gave me the strength and vision to write this book. I also thank God for the number of people He's placed along my path who have made a significant impact in my life. Although I can't mention everyone by name, I want to take a moment to thank a select group of people who played an instrumental role in my journey and have helped to make this book a reality.

First on my list is my family. My parents, Marian and James Jones Jr., are my heroes. Thank you for being there for every major step of my journey and always reminding me of the greatness inside of me. My sincere gratitude is also owed to my brother and sister-in-law, James and Hannah Jones, who have supported me in all of my ventures. I thank all of my aunts, uncles, cousins, and my older brother, Michael Jones, who have encouraged me to keep pressing forward toward my dream. In addition, I thank my godfather, Tony Jackson, and my late grandmother, Mattye Boone, for the seeds of faith they planted in my heart that are manifesting today.

I thank the Faith Community of St. Sabina for being my spiritual family and for the role they've played in developing my faith. I praise God for the staff and volunteers that I've had the opportunity to serve with for over eleven years at the ARK of St. Sabina, who gave their time, talents, and resources to make a difference in the lives of our youth. Special thanks is owed to my pastor, Father Michael Pfleger, whose teachings and passion for justice have inspired me to start my own ministry.

I want to thank my village at McCormick Theological Seminary, who not only provided me with the training I needed to write this book, but also serves as a vibrant faith community in my life that I can count on for spiritual guidance and encouragement. I am truly grateful for Tanya Davis, Sylvia Collins, and all of the other amazing women of Purpose By Design, who have inspired me to pursue my dreams so I can have a significant impact on this world.

I've also been surrounded by some amazing women and men of God, who I'm blessed to call my friends. I particularly want to thank those friends who have been there for me during the difficult seasons in my life, as well as those who helped me establish my ministry, Faith on the Journey. I want to thank my beloved girlfriends Marchonda Sanders and Jaime Williamson for being those women in my life who I can call on any time of day for prayer, guidance, and affirmation. My deepest appreciation also goes out to my dear friend Cynthia O'Brien, who played an instrumental role in my book writing process. In addition, I want to thank my accountability partner, Clarissa Christensen, who continuously uplifted me while writing this book. I would like to thank my friends Bruce Westfield, Tony Lawlor, Barbara Blair, Courtney Holmon, and Kristina Robison, who supported Faith on the Journey in its infancy stages, as well as my photographer, Michael Gunn, and the web design team at 773 Designs, who have partnered with me to move my vision forward.

Lastly, I would like to thank all of those people who have supported Faith on the Journey since its inception. Particularly, I want to thank those who had the courage to come forward and share their stories so that others can know that they're not alone. I would be remiss if I did not give special thanks to my friend Taliyba Reinberry, whose decision to tell her story through Faith on the Journey served as the inspiration for me writing this book. I pray that all of those named and unnamed who have loved and supported me along the way know that they will always hold a special place in my heart. May God continue to bless each and every one of you.

Introduction

From social media to plastic surgery to airbrushed images in magazines, it has become easier than ever before to hide our true selves from the world. But behind all of the smoke and mirrors, there is a lot more to people than what meets the eye. Since childhood, each of us has been trained in the art of wearing a mask. Often passed off as a self-preservation technique to prevent people from seeing what's really going on inside, we've learned how to shield others from discovering our insecurities, our fears, and our past pain. Simply put, to protect our genuine thoughts, feelings, and emotions—the very essence of who we are—we have put on a mask of deception. In doing so, we have lost the spirit of authenticity.

I discovered the magnitude of this problem when I launched my ministry called Faith on the Journey (FOTJ). I started FOTJ in 2018 after actively working in ministry for twelve years at St. Sabina Church and completing my first year in seminary school at McCormick Theological Seminary in Chicago, Illinois. I learned during my time in ministry that there were many Christians struggling in silence from the pain of their past. I wanted to use my background as a journalist, as well as the formal education I received from earning my M.A. in social work, to create a platform that would help people find emotional healing by sharing testimonies that demonstrated the faithfulness of God.

Within the first several months of my ministry, I interviewed dozens of people who had overcome significant trials in life, ranging from addiction, infertility, abandonment, abuse, loss of loved ones, and financial challenges—just to name a few. Hearing those heartfelt stories moved me deeply. Many of the people I interviewed had been emotionally tormented for decades by feelings of shame, anger, and grief from their past.

I was very familiar with these emotional handcuffs, as they had held me in bondage for years. How many people are harboring these feelings in silence? How many people do I interact with every day who are hiding their pain behind a mask? Those questions inspired me to write this book—a book for Christians struggling in silence from the pain of their past who desperately want to find freedom from its hold over their lives.

This book will:

- challenge you to uncover the pain you have hidden behind a mask and provide tangible steps to begin the healing process.

-shift your belief that the past has the ability to shape your future by empowering you to choose a life rooted in hope and driven by purpose.

-draw you closer to God by helping to remove barriers that prevent you from having an intimate relationship with Him.

-help you to identify ways in which God can use your past experiences to help others find freedom.

Throughout our journey together, I will share real stories of people who I've interviewed or encountered throughout my time in ministry. I will change the names of the individuals in the story to protect their identities but stay true to the important details of their experiences. I will also share glimpses of the process God has taken me through to remove my mask. It is my prayer that you see a part of yourself in each of these stories and recognize you are not alone.

I strongly encourage you to answer the reflection questions at the end of each chapter, as they will add significant value to your experience. Reference tools mentioned throughout the book can be found at breakingthemask.com.

I don't believe in coincidences. If you picked up this book, it is for a reason greater than you can ever imagine. God wants you to experience healing and freedom from your past, and I'm excited to be a part of that journey with you! Let us begin.

I was Given This Mask; I Didn't Make it

 "Life is a masquerade. Everywhere you look are people hiding behind masks."

-Ridze Khan

Tupac Shakur's 1993 hit song, "Keep Ya Head Up," sheds light on the ongoing struggles of inner-city life in the face of poverty, racism, and violence. While the song had an underlying message of hope, Shakur did not sugarcoat the harsh reality of being poor and black in America. Toward the latter half of his song, in response to some of the struggles of single mothers, he said, "Don't blame me. I was given this world; I didn't make it." Those words came to the forefront of my mind as I began to write this book. So many of us harbor pain in silence, beneath a mask given to us by the world.

This mask, like a physical one, is designed to deflect and hide. It prevents the outside world from seeing what lies underneath, but while shielding the exterior, it holds captive what is inside. It is the keeper of secrets and the master of illusions. The mask despises authenticity, fears transparency, and knows no vulnerability. The mask will stop at nothing to keep its image intact and emotions at bay. In its simplest form, the mask is the façade we project to the world.

The mask, which is constructed by society, says it is a sign of weakness to show emotion, it is best to avoid pain at all costs, and success is measured by fame and fortune. It is further perpetuated by a cyberworld that defines your value by the number of likes or follows you have on social media, as opposed to the content of your character. The mask of deception was finely sculpted before we ever entered into this world.

In other words, if you would allow me to remix the original version of Tupac Shakur's song, it would read, "Don't blame me. I was given this mask; I didn't make it."

It Starts When we are Young

Before many of us ever learned our ABCs, the mask became a familiar part of our wardrobe. A seemingly innocent example of this is often played out by loving parents attempting to get a good night's sleep. When their child barges into the room screaming about a monster in the closet, one of the half-awake parents may respond, "Stop being such a big baby. There's nothing to be afraid of. Just go back to bed." This emotionally invalidating response doesn't ease that child's fears—instead, it leaves them feeling rejected, ignored, and judged for having those fears.

Let's take this concept one step further. A six-year-old named Tim received a toy car from his grandmother right before she passed away. He loved that car more than anything and carried it with him everywhere—to school, to his tee-ball games, and even to bed. One day, after leaving an amusement park with his family, Tim realized he left the car inside the park. He immediately became frantic, desperate to go back inside the park to search for it—but the park was already closed.

Tim's eyes began to well up with water, but the second the first tear fell across his face, his dad yelled, "Real men don't cry. Toughen up. We'll get you another car."

Tim immediately collected himself, wiped his tears, and remained silent for the entire car ride home. That night, Tim was left questioning if it was wrong to feel sad for what happened. If he wasn't wrong to feel sad, he realized it must be wrong to *express* how he feels. The father in this story not only invalidated Tim's feelings, but he began to shape Tim's definition of masculinity as one that does not have room for showing emotions. In essence, Tim's father began the process of molding Tim's mask. Similar responses, such as "Why are you crying?" (if made in a judgmental tone) or "You're okay," (dismissing their feelings) can also add layers to a person's mask.

Boys and men are not the only ones who have adopted the false belief that crying is a sign of weakness. I have apologized many times for crying in front of people as an adult. The fact that I allowed them to see this vulnerable side of me was embarrassing and in direct contrast with this mask of strength I wanted to portray. As a rising leader in my profession, I also had to be careful not to come across as an "overemotional" or "sensitive" woman. Like many of us, I believed exemplifying this image of confidence, success, and "having it all together" was the standard I should seek to attain—even if, behind closed doors, my life was in shambles.

. . .

Media and the Masquerade

We shouldn't be surprised that the mask has become a staple accessory in our lives, considering we are inundated with messages on social media that reinforce we should only display images of joy, fun, and excitement to the world. Nine times out of ten your Facebook and Instagram feed are flooded with perfectly-modeled selfies, people partying, couples madly in love, and travelers living their "best life." If we compare ourselves to what we see other people doing on social media, our lives look pathetic. From the outside, it seems like no one else has real problems.

Social media has become an online, 24-hour, masquerade event. We are able to come in and out of the party whenever we want, strategically choosing which aspects of ourselves we would like to reveal to the world. We feel there is no way we can ever let the world know what is really going on behind our masks. However, when we log off, the parts of our stories left untold still must be dealt with.

Now, let's imagine you and I found ourselves stuck in a masquerade alternate universe that was not a digital reality, but our real lives. An existence where we couldn't log off from the outside world. A place where we constantly felt forced to perform, to dress perfectly, to never gain any weight or have a bad day out of fear the paparazzi will reveal what we really have going on inside. I'm quite sure that's how celebrities feel, as their fame and fortune has come at a price.

We've seen countless examples of celebrities who seemed to "have it all," only to discover they're struggling just like you and me with pain, shame, and the heartaches of this world. Grammy award-winning artist Lady Gaga's energy and confidence are magnetic on stage, but she struggles with anxiety and depression when she removes her mask at home.[1] Robert Downey Jr., one of the highest-paid actors of all time, struggled behind his mask for years with an addiction to drugs.[2] Musical icons such as Whitney Houston, Michael Jackson, and Prince have all left this world too soon as a result of drug overdoses, and the tragic suicide of Kate Spade left us wondering what pain a woman who possessed such beauty, wealth, and fame harbored in silence behind her mask.

Time Doesn't Heal all Wounds

I discovered the power of the mask during a conversation with a friend of mine. Sheila was held captive by her mask for over thirty years. She described to me in vivid detail a series of traumatic events she endured as a child and young adult. Sheila lived in a foster home, and she vividly remembers discussing with her little brother whether or not they should tell their foster parents that someone was molesting them. They were ashamed of what happened but knew it was wrong to keep it a secret.

Sheila finally built up enough courage to talk to their foster parents. She immediately felt a weight lift. She just knew that they would take action and help her move forward from this experience.

Sadly, Sheila was wrong. After the initial conversation, Sheila's foster parents thought it best to never discuss the incident again.

"There was no follow-up. It was as if it never happened," Sheila remembered.

Her foster mother told her, "Time heals all wounds," and things would get better, but they didn't. Her wound instead became deeper when Sheila was molested again a few years later. Sheila learned from her first experience the best response to pain was to sweep it under the rug, so Sheila did just that. She remained quiet and put on a mask to cover up layers of shame, embarrassment, and pain. Although the mask was able to hide Sheila's pain, it didn't stop the pain from steering her down a dark road of abuse and self-hatred. She remained in an abusive relationship for years and did not tell a soul, assuming her pain would be dismissed or ignored again. Sheila survived that abusive relationship, but it took years for her to begin peeling back the layers of shame that had consumed her life. It was only when Sheila finally found the courage to remove the mask that her healing began.

Sheila's story represents the silent voices of countless other children in this world who were told to bury their pain behind a mask. We learn from her story that there are many of us who operate out of a misconception that ignoring a problem exempts us from having to decide how to handle that problem. However, our choice to ignore an issue is *still making a decision*—a decision that will undoubtedly lead to more pain, damage, and despair.

The Effects of the Mask on the World

Don't believe me? Well, let's look at some statistics:

- According to the Center for Disease Control and Prevention (CDC), a total of 70,237 drug overdose deaths occurred in the United States in 2017. The age-adjusted rate of overdose deaths increased significantly by 9.6 percent from 2016 (19.8 per 100,000) to 2017 (21.7 per 100,000). [3]
- The CDC reported 1 in 6, or 37 million, adults binge

drink about once a week, consuming an average of seven drinks per binge. Binge drinking is defined as consuming five or more drinks for men, or four or more drinks for women, in about two hours. Annually, binge drinking is responsible for more than half of the 88,000 alcohol-attributable deaths. [4]

- The National Coalition Against Domestic Violence reports that 1 in 3 women and 1 in 4 men have experienced some form of physical violence by an intimate partner. [5]
- The Anxiety and Depression Association of America reports that there are 6.8 million adults (3.1 percent) diagnosed with an anxiety disorder, 16.1 million American adults (6.7 percent) were diagnosed with Major Depression Disorder. [6]
- The CDC reported a total of 47,173 Americans died from suicide in 2017. [7]

Do you see a problem here? Although I would be remiss not to acknowledge mental illness's influence on some of these statistics, I'm also convinced many people who are physically violent or struggle with addiction, depression, or other chronic disorders are attempting to mask pain.

We've become masters of performing in front of people like everything is okay, when in reality we are dying inside. We respond to a coworker's greeting with the robotic, "I'm fine," when the truth is our dog just died and our boss gave us the pink slip. Maybe if we knew people genuinely cared and wouldn't judge us, we would respond differently, but society has conditioned us to assume otherwise.

· · ·

The Faith Community and the Mask

This interaction is not any better in the faith community. The all-too-common sayings, "I'm too blessed to be stressed," and "I'm too blessed to be depressed," has so many of us lying. We know we just had an argument with our spouse last night, our kids are out of control, and we barely have enough money to pay our electricity bill. Let's just be honest. "I'm blessed, but I'm *stressed*!"

We can become so focused on projecting an image of holiness that we are prevented from connecting and relating to those around us. The other side of that coin becomes evident when someone in church shares their struggles with grief, shame, or loss, and is met with, "Just have faith," or "God will work it out." Yes, I believe faith is important, and I am convinced God *will* work things out—however, moments when people are in deep despair and are attempting to remove their mask to show you how they really feel are not the time to share Christian colloquialism. What they are looking for is someone to support them in their pain and acknowledge their feelings are valid.

If you have realized that you have been wearing a mask, you are definitely not alone. The mask has become a garment of comfort for many of us. Believe me, I understand how scary and difficult removing the mask can be. "What would people really think about me if they knew the truth?" or "Am I strong enough to face what happened to me?" are common questions that will surface for many of us during this process. However, choosing to continue burying pain behind the mask is not the answer. Although the choice is yours, I've learned to look at buried pain like a seed. It grows like a weed. We can prune it, cut it down, and even learn to live with it for a while, but until we destroy the root, it will keep growing back.

God is With us During This Process

God desires to go to the root of our pain and help us extract any weeds that stand in the way of us living the life that He has called us to have—for the God we serve "heals the brokenhearted and bandages their wounds" (Psalm 147:3). As a Christian who full-heartedly believes in the healing power of God, I am 100 percent convinced God does not want us to live a life held captive by the pain of our past. He wants us to live a life of significant purpose.

Scripture tells us in Jeremiah 29:11, "For I know the plans I have for you...plans to prosper you and not to harm you, plans to give you hope and a future." Even with this promise, God did not tell us we would go through life without experiencing dark days. God's beloved Job, who was blameless in His sight, experienced significant hardship and pain. Jesus's disciples were under constant criticism and attack, many eventually losing their lives for their faith in Jesus. The Lord our God experienced pain watching his only son die on a cross. Pain is a part of life, and that is something we cannot avoid.

However, God promises that He will be with us during those dark days. "For I, the Lord your God, will hold your right hand, saying to you, 'Fear not, I will help you'" (Isaiah 41:13). This is a promise we must stand on, knowing He will see us through difficult moments in our lives. We must believe we are blessed and that every breath we take serves as evidence that God still has an assignment for us to fulfill.

There is freedom available beyond the mask, and it is my

prayer that this book will help you discover it. We are going to take a deep, hard look at the ways unresolved pain has held us back in our lives, and we will work to identify the mask that has been used to cover it up. We will then explore ways in which we can break the power that these masks have had over our lives. We will analyze the psychological dynamics at play and look at what is taking place from a spiritual perspective. Our first step is to explore the source of your pain.

Chapter 1 Reflection

Key Point: Avoiding our pain is not the answer. We must allow God to get to the root of our pain so He can heal it.

Question to Consider: What are sayings you've heard or experiences you've had in your past that have helped to shape your mask?

Scripture to Remember: "He heals the brokenhearted and bandages their wounds." (Psalm 147:3 NLT)

I'm Stuck in a Pain Pit

 "We are products of our past, but we don't have to be prisoners of it."

-Rick Warren

Once while picking up take-out, my eyes locked on a car that had jumped the curb by the parking lot exit. Being the "good Christian" I am, I had every intention to mind my own business and keep on walking—but when I got close enough to the scene, I realized it was someone I knew from church named Tina. Tina's rear passenger-side tire was lodged into a deep dirt pit. Every time Tina pressed the gas, the back wheels turned aggressively, but there was no movement. When Tina saw me, she greeted me with a smile and hello, but her attention quickly reverted back to the situation at hand.

A fellow onlooker and I decided to help. We pushed the car with all our might while she hit the gas, but we soon realized our pitiful attempt was only driving the tire farther into the ground. We were getting nowhere, and Tina was getting flustered. Luckily, our situation caught the eye of a mechanic that happened to be passing by.

He said, "Man, that tire is really stuck in there good."

I thought to myself, *No kidding, genius!*

The mechanic explained there was no way that we could push a rear wheel in this position out on our own. He told us we needed to call a tow truck company for assistance, because if we continued pushing the car, we were going to cause serious damage to the bottom of the vehicle. In other words, we needed to rely on a source that was beyond our own strength to help us get out of the pit.

Like Tina, we often find ourselves frustrated by pits of pain. When we endure an extremely traumatic experience, it is easy to feel as if we are held captive by the pain from our past with no idea how to escape it. We might attempt to get out of that pain pit with our own strength, but in doing so, we only cause more damage to ourselves. This is why we need a power greater than ourselves to help us out of the pit. We need God.

Seek Healing From the One who Made us

God is our manufacturer. We are born into this world like a brand-new car, but as time progresses, the experiences we have on our journey begin to beat us up. We might experience an accident on the road, drive over an unexpected pothole, or get stuck in an unexpected hailstorm. After a while, the car has experienced some significant damages that are in need of repair, some of which are invisible to the naked eye.

To save money, we can go to the alley mechanic down the street, but because they don't know our car as well as the manufacturer, they might put a foreign part on our vehicle that can completely damage the engine. We can choose to ignore the damage altogether and just pray the car continues to work, but the initial problem will cause other issues. We can try to spiff up the car on the outside with shiny rims and a new paint job, but inside, that car is still broken.

When it comes to the damaged places in our hearts, we must recognize that our only option for true healing is God. God knows everything about us—our insecurities, our fears, our hopes, our struggles, and the underlying sources of our pain. Scripture tells us that before God formed us in the womb, He knew us (Jeremiah 1:5), and He knows every hair on our head (Matthew 10:30). He wants to help us out of our pit of despair, but many times we've decided instead to run to friends, ignore the problem, or mask the pain. These actions are just causing more damage inside. The only way we can get out of our pain pits is through the grace of God.

What is Happening Inside our Minds?

Let's take a moment to break down how pain pits work. These pain pits, from a neurological standpoint, can be very difficult to escape. Dr. Joe Dispenza, a world-renowned doctor and scientist, described in an interview on the Ed Mylett show about Impact Theory, how our brains are like a memory bank. When we have a traumatic experience, our brains store a snapshot of that experience in our long-term memory. Well, afterward, our bodies continue to signal to us to pay attention because they want us to be prepared in case that event happens again. Eventually, if this process happens enough, our bodies become hardwired to live in survival mode. In other words, our bodies have learned to respond without us. [1]

I remember driving to work one day. I approached a train track, and the car in front of me came to a complete stop before proceeding over the track. I slammed on my brakes and was able to stop in time, but the car behind me didn't. They rear-ended me. Thankfully, the accident wasn't severe; but ever since that moment, every time I have to make an abrupt stop, I immediately cringe and look back in my rearview mirror as if someone is going to hit me from behind. My body has been conditioned to respond based on a negative experience I had in the past. This is how many of us are living our lives. We survived something traumatic in our past, but our bodies remain on fight-or-flight mode in an effort to protect ourselves from a potential threat.

Fight or flight, also known as acute stress response, is a physiological reaction in the face of something that is physically or mentally terrifying. When our bodies sense danger, they triggers hormones that prepare us to either deal with the threat by fighting or run away to safety. While in this state, our bodies release catecholamines—which include noradrenaline and adrenaline—that cause our blood pressure, heart rate, and breathing rate to increase. God made our bodies this way to allow us to protect ourselves when we are in danger, but the problem is our bodies can respond this way when there isn't an actual threat. [2]

The way our bodies are wired, they don't know the difference between an actual threat and one that we've made up in our minds. If we continue to anticipate the worst possible scenario for our future based on past experiences, we're beginning to condition our minds to operate in a state of fear. If we do that long enough, our bodies will begin to have a panic attack without us having any control over it. This is the primary reason adults have anxiety attacks, rooted in something that happened in their childhood. Sadly, this means they have not been able to change since that event. *They are stuck* and need help moving forward. [3]

Getting out of the Pain Pit

Pain pits—or, as they're considered in the spiritual realm, strongholds—are what the devil uses to keep us locked in a mental prison, away from the freedom and joy God wants to give us. We have to learn to recognize Satan and his tactics. In doing so, we must accept that wearing masks to hide our pain pits from others will not get us out of our situation. Instead of hiding, we must come before God seeking what rightfully belongs to us. The Bible says, "But he was pierced for our transgressions, he was crushed for our iniquities; the punishment that brought us peace was on him, and by his wounds we are healed" (Isaiah 53:5). God is our healer, but we have to exercise our faith to receive what is promised to us.

Now, this truth doesn't negate that God can use people (i.e., counselors, friendships, support groups) or medication to help us. However, let's be clear that God will use them as *resources*, but He will always be the *source* of our healing. "For everything comes from him and exists by his power and is intended for his glory. All glory to him forever! Amen" (Romans 11:36 NLT). In other words, God has equipped humans to create the tools we use in our daily lives, just like He will strategically place people along our path to support us. God is at the center of every good work, so when we experience our healing, all glory belongs to Him.

We also must understand that emotional healing does not

mean God will delete our memories, nor can we expect that we will never have another emotional response to our past pain. The type of healing I'm speaking of means gaining the ability to voice our pain and not remain stuck in it. It means embracing joy, peace, anger, and sadness in the way God intended, rather than experiencing our present circumstances only through the lens of past pain. The healing that we seek means being able to receive God's unconditional love with an understanding that we are defined by our Creator, not our past. Our healing means having an incomprehensible hope in the one True God who will never leave or forsake us. If I were to define this emotional healing in one word, it would be "peace."

God reminds us in his Word, "not to be anxious about anything, but in every situation, by prayer and petition, with thanksgiving, present your requests to God. And the *peace* of God, which transcends all understanding, will guard your hearts and your minds in Christ Jesus" (Philippians 4:6–7 NIV). This peace is available to us, but we must believe it and seek it fullheartedly from God.

The Journey Ahead

Before moving forward, I must warn you up front that this is not about avoiding pain. Pain is a part of life, and can often serve as a catalyst for growth. It is my intention to help change your relationship with pain, so when you do experience it, you know how to interact with it and don't get stuck there.

It is also important to note that I will reference real life examples of people who have been stuck in their pain. I caution you to refrain from comparing the severity of your pain to theirs. Comparing one's pain to someone else's is unfair and can be a major hindrance to our growth. I learned this lesson during a conversation with a professional body-builder, Christine. This woman, who was about 5'8 and 125 pounds soaking wet, shared her experiences preparing for a competition. At the time, I was still pretty new to weightlift-ing, and I remember telling her my one rep max for a deadlift was not nearly as much as other people I knew. Immediately, she stopped me in my tracks.

"It doesn't matter if you're a 300-pound guy deadlifting 400 or a 130-pound woman deadlifting 150," Christine said. "The bar feels the same…heavy!"

This simple truth could be applied to so many different areas of our lives. When it comes to our pain, heavy is heavy. When we try to measure our pain against someone else's, it leads to judgement and prevents us from being able to minister to others or receive support when we're hurting. Resist the temptation to compare. We are all more alike than different. So let's take this journey toward healing together.

I've found in my years of ministry three main pain pits that have caused people to become stuck: shame, unforgive-ness, and grief. We will focus our attention on exploring those pain pits individually, then identify how they are each in rela-tionship with the mask.

Chapter 2 Reflection

Key Point: Emotional healing is not forgetting what happened to us. It's being able to receive God's unconditional love and fully embracing all of the emotions that God gave us versus experiencing life through the lens of our past.

Questions to Consider: Is there one negative experience that has happened in your past that you continue to think about and fear happening again? How has that fear affected your life?

Scripture to Remember: "But he was pierced for our transgressions, he was crushed for our iniquities; the punishment that brought us peace was on him, and by his wounds we are healed." (Isaiah 53:5 NIV)

Shame: I Can't get Past What I've Done

 "Shame says that, 'Because I am flawed, I am unacceptable.' Grace says that, 'Though I am flawed, I am cherished.'"

-Michelle Graham

I define shame as a belief we are not good enough and that God's grace is not big enough to cover our imperfections. As Christians, many of us struggle with shame because there is a part of us that has not fully embraced the power of the redemption story which tells us God sacrificed his only son to cover *all* our sins—past, present, and future. As a result of this act of love, God opened the door for us to enter into a full relationship with Him. Shame, however, serves as a barrier to that. When we sin, shame shifts our focus to what we've done wrong instead of shifting our focus to God's ability to redeem, restore, and cleanse us from the sins of our past. If we fall into the pain pit of shame, it can eventually lead us to believe we are not worthy of God's love, and we can find ourselves drifting away from our faith.

A friend of mine named Jeff shared with me his experiences with shame. Jeff has always been known by everyone for his strong Christian values. Since he gave his life to God in his early 20s, he had sought to live a righteous life and believed in abstaining from sex until marriage. He remained celibate for years, but eventually entered into a relationship with a woman who was a Christian but didn't share the same values as him. She thought waiting until marriage was crazy and pressured Jeff to have sex with her. Finally, Jeff gave in. He felt guilty at first, but after a while began to enjoy it. Then his girlfriend got pregnant. Jeff was mortified. He feared his decision would not only cost him his leadership position in church, but it would also affect his witness to other Christians. Jeff eventually stopped attending church because he felt guilty for breaking his promise to God. What was even harder to deal with was the shame he felt from letting his community at the church down.

Like Jeff, we've all made wrong turns and found ourselves stuck in the pain pit of shame. Shame has the ability to paralyze us and can linger in our lives for years if we allow it. The feeling of shame is often described in relation to guilt, so before going any further, I want to define the distinct difference between these two words.

Guilt and Conviction

Let's start by taking a good hard look at guilt. The Greek word in the new testament for guilt is *enochos*, which means "liable, accountable"; *opheilo*, which means "debt, obligation"; and *aitia*, "grounds for punishment." When we step out of the will of God, we are guilty (liable, have grounds for punishment) of committing a wrongdoing.[1]

God speaks to us about our wrongdoings, through the Holy Spirit, by *convicting* us. The Hebrew word for conviction is *yakah*, which means "to argue with, to prove, and to correct."[2] The Holy Spirit's job is to convict us by convincing us that we have done wrong and we need to turn to God in repentance. This could be likened to an attorney making the case that the defendant has committed a crime. When this comes to our attention, we will feel guilty because we are in fact guilty of a sin that caused us to separate ourselves from God.

Now, the devil, who always attempts to distort anything God created, will sometimes attempt to impede "false guilt" on us for actions we might have taken that were not wrong or were simply out of our control. For example, we can feel guilty for being in a car accident that we had no control over, or a child can feel guilty for their pet goldfish dying under their care. As a person becomes more familiar with God's love and the truth of His Word, they will become less susceptible to falling into false guilt.

We can have a healthy experience with guilt by acknowledging that we have sinned and engaging in the act of repentance by asking God for forgiveness and turning away from our sin. After that takes place, it is not God's will for us to remain in this state of guilt because Jesus already paid the price for our sins. For example, let's imagine when we commit a sin, the Holy Spirit comes knocking at our door. The Holy Spirit comes to *convict* us by handing us an important letter that says we've done something wrong that needs to be fixed, which creates this feeling of guilt inside of us. Michael Lewis, PhD in clinical and experimental psychology, notes that this interaction is intended to provoke us to stop, signaling that what we have done is in violation of a standard or rule, thereby prompting us to change our behavior.[3]

The feeling of guilt is designed to generate some sort of anxiety inside of us in order to cause us to take action. It is similar to the function that pain plays in our lives. When someone's body is attacked by a disease, pain begins to surface in different areas of that person's body as a signal that something is wrong that needs to be fixed. The same thing applies to guilt. Whenever we commit a sin, God convicts us by pricking at our heart by way of the Holy Spirit and telling us that our actions were a sin against Him or our fellow man, and we need to fix it.

Guilt is never meant to stay as a long-term guest. Once the Holy Spirit accomplished its mission, the feeling of guilt is meant to pack up its things and hit the road. However, as that feeling of guilt is trying to head out, Satan is anxiously looking for a small opening in which he could sneak his two-legged helpers into your house to wreak havoc.

Condemnation and Shame

The first unwelcome guest is Condemnation. Condemnation is a response to our sin that is in complete opposition to God's response. Instead of coming to our house to tell us, "Hey, you need to clean up this mess," Condemnation is going to say, "Hey, your house is a mess, just like you!" One of Satan's names is "Accuser of the Brethren." He loves to stand before God and us reminding us of our failures. The enemy wants to do nothing more than roll a big-screen TV into our house with a video of our sins looping over and over again. If we let him, he will plop down on the couch with some popcorn to enjoy seeing us in utter turmoil as we watch that video replay in our mind. Then, while prompting us to relive what we did, the enemy continues whispering in our ear that we are no good, that we will just fall into that same sin again and that what we've done is unforgivable. Once Satan has convinced us of all this, he has set the stage for the second unwanted guest to enter the room: Shame.

When Shame enters the house, it likes to leave the door wide open behind it, saying, "Now everyone on the street can see your messy house, too." Shame, at its root, is invoked by our negative perception of how we appear to others and ourselves. Unlike Guilt, whose job is to tell you, "Pay attention to what you are doing because it is not good," Shame says, "*You* are no good."[4] While Guilt is a focus on behavior, Shame is a focus on self. Brené Brown, PhD, who has conducted research on shame for over two decades, said, "Guilt is, 'I did something bad.' Shame is, 'I am bad.' Guilt: 'I'm sorry. I made a mistake.' Shame: 'I'm sorry. I am a mistake.'"[5] Like Guilt, Shame can be felt when we've done nothing wrong, such as the shame that comes with physical, mental, or sexual abuse. Shame also causes us to believe that others think we are damaged, unworthy, or unlovable.

In Nathaniel Hawthorne's 1850 novel, *The Scarlet Letter*, a woman named Hester had a child out of wedlock. When her secret came out, she was forced to wear a scarlet letter "A" on her breast for adultery. Those of us who are suffering from Shame are living as if we have a scarlet letter on our chest. No matter what we change or how hard we pray, we can't seem to rid ourselves of the Shame that comes with this scarlet letter. Hester was given the scarlet letter to make her believe her identity was her sin. She committed adultery, so she is an adulterer, and that is all. The devil wants us to believe that what we have done or have experienced is who we are. If we had an abortion, we're a murderer. If we committed fraud, we're a thief. If we went to prison, we're a criminal. If we've been abused, we're damaged. The world might try to label us as simply that, but that's not who we are.

Our Identity is in Christ

Imagine that what caused you to feel shame is the small dot in the middle of the big circle (Figure A). The large circle around that small dot represents every other aspect of our lives that make up who we are, from our personality, the service we do in the community, the children or parents we care for, and the talents that we bring into this world. Shame has the ability to cause us to focus solely on that small little dot, magnifying it to the point where when we look in the mirror, that's all we see. In reality, there is so much more around that tiny little dot that makes up who we are. Now, let's point our attention to the box the big circle is surrounded by. This box represents Jesus Christ. As believers, it is important to understand our identity as believers (the circle) is *in* Christ (the box).

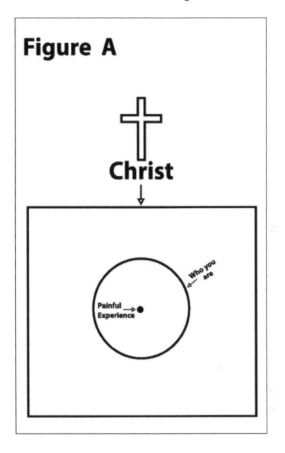

No matter what happens to us inside the circle, our identity will never change because we will always be children of God. We can also find joy in knowing that His love for us is not based on our performance as Christians, but is unconditional. The Bible says that "neither death nor life, neither angels nor demons, neither the present nor the future, nor any powers, neither height nor depth, nor anything else in all creation, will be able to separate us from the love of God that is in Christ Jesus our Lord" (Romans 8:38–39). Do you really understand what that scripture is saying? *Nothing*, including our worst sins, can separate us from God's love. Now, this doesn't mean we won't have to face repercussions for our sins. When we make the decision to step out of the will of God, the consequences can be costly. However, it will never change God's desire to be in relationship with us.

As we gain a deeper knowledge of our true identity, it helps us to become better equipped to fight against the attacks of the enemy. We must recognize that Satan will not go down without a fight. The weapons of shame and condemnation that Satan uses against us should not be taken lightly, but know we have the power and authority to overcome all of Satan's evil ploys. We know from our faith that condemnation and shame were both dealt with on the cross when Jesus died for us. They do not have the power to control us unless we allow them to. We have the choice to fight back, and our weapon is the Word of God.

The Bible describes the Word as a sword (Ephesians 6:17) and refers to our faith as a shield (Ephesians 6:16) that protects us from the attacks of evil. As our faith grows stronger, it is able to help shield us from falling victim to the attacks of the enemy. When Satan tries to tell us who we are, we can respond back with what the Word of God says about who we are. When the enemy says, "You're dirty," we can respond back, "The Lord calls me the apple of His eye." When the devil says, "You're worthless," we can proclaim, "The Lord calls me His friend." When Satan says, "You will not be able to recover from your past," we will shout, "I'm more than a conqueror through Christ Jesus."

Study the Word, know who you are in Christ, believe that God has marked you for His purpose, and accept no other label than Child of God.

Chapter 3 Reflection

Key Point: Our identity is not defined by what we've done or what has happened to us. Our identity is based on who we are, which is a child of God.

Questions to Consider: What is an experience you've had where you felt like people looked down upon you because of what happened or would judge you if they became aware of what took place? Has that experience continued to shape how your view yourself today?

Scripture to Remember: "There is therefore now no condemnation to them which are in Christ Jesus, who walk not after the flesh, but after the Spirit." (Romans 8:1 KJV)

Unforgiveness: I Can't get Past What You've Done to Me

 "To forgive is to set a prisoner free and discover that the prisoner was you."

-Lewis B. Smedes

I remember a time early in my 20s, when I was appointed the head of a ministry at my church. The other people I served with often emphasized how young I was in their congratulatory remarks, especially a woman named Jackie. Jackie was older and had a lot of experience in ministry, so she offered to support me as I entered into the new role.

At first, I believed Jackie genuinely had my best interest at heart and would serve as a trusted mentor, but it didn't take long before I realized she was trying to use me to advance her own personal agenda. The signs came in small ways. First, I noticed she was working on tasks that were not assigned to her, but when I asked her about it, she said she was just taking on additional responsibilities to help. Then I started to recognize certain things Jackie said weren't adding up. One day, God prompted me to "fact-check" the information Jackie shared with me. I discovered Jackie had lied to me on a number of occasions to cover up the fact she was spending money on unauthorized expenses. She had also set out to defame my character to other members of the ministry by spreading rumors about me and telling others I wasn't qualified for the position. To make matters worse, when I confronted her about the situation, she met me with tears and hostility. Her plea of innocence was Oscar-worthy. I was livid and felt so betrayed. Even after she decided to leave the ministry, the residue from that experience stayed with me well beyond that moment.

I resented Jackie for breaking my trust. Any time someone brought up her name, I immediately became infuriated. It was so bad that whenever I saw her name on a document, random expletives would start flying out of my mouth (I'm saved, but God is still working on me.). Initially, I thought my bitterness was only directed toward Jackie, but I was wrong. As a result of my experience with Jackie, I developed serious trust issues. The anger I allowed to fester in my heart began to change my disposition and how I looked at people. I no longer entered into relationships with an open mind, thinking the best of people. My guard was up against everyone I worked with in ministry. I found myself giving individuals who I served with the "side eye," constantly double-checking behind them. I needed to be in control of every situation so no one would ever have a chance to "burn me" again.

During that season, I had fallen into the unforgiveness pain pit with no intentions of escaping. God had to do some major work on my heart to help me forgive Jackie, and it didn't happen overnight.

· · ·

Why Should we Forgive?

The process began when God helped me gain an understanding of why we should forgive in the first place. In a conversation Peter had with Jesus in the Bible, he asked, "Lord, how many times shall I forgive my brother when he sins against me? Up to seven times?" Jesus answered, "I tell you, not seven times, but seventy-seven times" (Matthew 18:21–22). When I first read that scripture, I honestly felt like Jesus was being a little unreasonable. I mean, does He just want those who harm us to keep running us over? On the surface, it seems as if we are letting those who hurt us "off the hook," but I've come to learn that no one ever gets away with sin. Though we might never have the opportunity to see the consequences of another person's sin, God sees everything. The Bible tells us that we serve a just God. Those who harm us have to answer to Him for their sins. It is not our place to try to step into the role of God to seek revenge ourselves. On the contrary, God wants us to forgive those who harm us—not just for them, but for us. I once read a quote from an unknown author that says, "Forgiveness doesn't excuse their behavior. Forgiveness prevents their behavior from destroying your heart." We must learn to protect our heart at all cost, because everything we do flows from it (Proverbs 4:23).

We cannot allow ourselves to get stuck in unforgiveness. It will undoubtedly hinder and complicate our daily walk with God. Our fellowship with God flows freely when we operate in love, but as soon as unforgiveness takes root in our spirit, that fellowship is disrupted. Satan loves when that happens because it gives him a small opening to enter in and tempt us to sin. That's why the Bible warns us in 2 Corinthians 2:10–11, that "Anyone you forgive, I also forgive.

35

And what I have forgiven—if there was anything to forgive—I have forgiven in the sight of Christ for your sake, in order that Satan might not outwit us. For we are not unaware of his schemes." When we don't forgive, we are helping Satan torture us. We must be savvy to how the devil uses unforgiveness against us, so we don't fall victim to it.

Carrying unforgiveness in our heart also negatively impacts our prayers with God. We see this in Mark 11:22–25 (ESV):

And Jesus answered them, "Have faith in God. Truly, I say to you, whoever says to this mountain, 'Be taken up and thrown into the sea,' and does not doubt in his heart, but believes that what he says will come to pass, it will be done for him. Therefore I tell you, whatever you ask in prayer, believe that you have received it, and it will be yours. And whenever you stand praying, forgive, if you have anything against anyone, so that your Father also who is in heaven may forgive you your trespasses."

In Jesus's teaching about faith and the power of prayer, He made it a point to tell us we must forgive anyone that has done wrong against us. When we do this, it allows us to share in the unmerited love we received from Christ who has forgiven us first. It is important for us to recognize that God is not asking us to do anything He hasn't done for us already. Andy Stanley, founder of the worldwide Christian organization called North Point Ministries, once said, "In the shadow of my hurt, forgiveness feels like a decision to reward my enemy, but in the shadow of the cross, forgiveness is merely a gift from one undeserving soul to another."[1] Stanley's statement is rooted in an understanding that we are all sinners who live in a fallen world. Although someone else's sin may seem worse than ours, in God's eyes each sin is all the same.

For that reason, we are commissioned by God to release those who have harmed us from the bonds of unforgiveness.

I Can't Forgive Unless They Apologize to Me

In previous conversations I've had with people about forgiveness, I've heard people express they will only forgive someone if they ask for forgiveness. Although I value the role that repentance plays in the reconciliation process, I think that stance is flawed. Say, for instance, a boy named John grew up in a house with his mother and his two younger sisters. His dad was in and out of jail his entire life, and when he wasn't serving time in prison, he was out on the streets either selling drugs or gambling. The only interactions John ever had with his dad were negative. His dad always called him "soft" and told him he would never be good enough. John *hated* his dad for not being there for his family and for treating him like he was nothing his entire life. The last interaction he had with his dad ended in a fight, during which John told his dad he wished he were dead. John vowed he would never forgive him. From that day forward, John never spoke of his dad again.

Although John went on to become highly successful, he had significant anger issues that surfaced in all of his relationships. When John was 26, he got a call from his sister that his father died in a car accident. John seemed almost numb from the news. He didn't care, nor did he want to go to the funeral, but his sister begged him to come. At the funeral, John met one of his father's estranged sisters for the first time. She shared with him that John's father had been physically, mentally, and sexually abused his entire childhood. That's why they both fled from home. When his dad was living on the streets, he ended up involved in a gang and got addicted to drugs. John was shocked when he heard the news and left the funeral torn up inside. He hated his father for all those years, but felt for the first time a bit of compassion because of what he experienced as a child. John's dad never had the opportunity to apologize for what he had done, but John still had a choice to make. Would he continue to hold resentment in his heart toward his dad, or would he forgive him?

John's story brings up a number of major points. We learned that John's father was acting out of his state of brokenness. Often, negative behavior on the surface is only a reflection of a deeper pain within. John's father masked his past trauma from his son by acting out in anger, which ultimately ruined their relationship. If John knew his dad's full story, it probably wouldn't have made his childhood easier, but it would have possibly helped him to understand.

If someone broke into your car and stole your money, you would be angry. However, if you found out that the person only broke into your car so they could buy food to feed their children, in spite of your pain, a part of you would feel a sense of compassion toward them. We will never know the full story behind someone's negative choices or their pain, which is why God is always pushing us to respond in love to one another.

The resentment John held in his heart toward his dad was negatively affecting his quality of life. If John held on to the belief that he could only forgive a person if they apologize, then John's peace just went into the grave with his father. The forgiveness in this scenario is not for his dad. The forgiveness in this story is for John. The harsh reality is we might not ever receive the apology we deserve from the person that has harmed us, but we cannot give that person the power to keep us yoked in chains of unforgiveness for the rest of our lives. We must learn to let go and forgive those who have done us wrong. This doesn't mean that we need to stay in a relationship with them. It doesn't mean that we should continue to allow them to mistreat us. It just means that we seek to demonstrate God's love toward them through the act of forgiveness.

Making the Choice to Forgive

Forgiving is an action which boils down to a choice that we make. This biblical truth is confirmed by one of our greatest leaders in the Bible: Joseph (Genesis 37–50). Joseph had every reason to be angry at the world. His own brothers sold Joseph into slavery, then he was sent to jail under false allegations by the guard captain's wife. Yet, in the midst of all that, God never left Joseph's side. After years of imprisonment, God elevated Joseph to a position of Vizier, second in command of the nation. Then, Joseph's brothers who sold him into slavery begged him not to seek revenge on them and to help them in their time of need. Joseph could have easily responded, "Um, it's payback time, suckers!" but his response was the exact opposite of that. He said to them, "You intended to harm me, but God intended it for good to accomplish what is now being done, the saving of many lives" (Genesis 50:20).

Wow! How powerful is that?! I must admit, I don't know if my initial response would have been as gracious as Joseph's. Joseph, in his maturity, was able to see beyond the pain and hurt that he endured and look at his situation from God's perspective. He didn't spend his time ruminating on what his brothers had done to him. Joseph chose to look at how God was able to use his circumstances to save lives. That revelation is huge! Think about how that paradigm shift could be an absolute game-changer in our lives. What if God says, "I know that this person has done you wrong, but the pain that you experienced from them will not go in vain. I will use every tear you've cried as the fuel needed to birth a ministry, a nonprofit, or a movement that changes public policy so that the lives of countless other people can be saved or changed because of your works." God shines through the darkest of situations all the time.

We've seen this in recent years through the life of Nelson Mandela. He was imprisoned and brutally tortured by his oppressors for 27 years. Yet, when he got out of prison and became president of South Africa, he invited one of the jailers who tortured him to the inauguration. Mandela had a deep understanding of the power of forgiveness. When asked about his experience, he said, "As I walked out of the door toward the gate that would lead to my freedom, I knew if I didn't leave my bitterness and hatred behind, I'd still be in prison." [2]

Like Mandela, we must choose to not allow the hurt and pain we've experienced keep us stuck in a pain pit. We must embrace the fact that what happened in the past does not have the final say concerning the person who harmed us or ourselves. Although we cannot erase what they've done, we can make a decision not to allow their past harms to dictate our future.

Chapter 4 Reflection

Key Point: Forgiveness is a choice that we make that not only benefits the one that is in need of forgiveness, but it also keeps our hearts free of bitterness, resentment, and other strongholds of the enemy.

Questions to Consider: Is there someone from your past who has let you down or has deeply hurt you that you struggle to forgive? If so, acknowledge the pain they have caused and ask God to help heal the broken places of your heart from that experience. Then seek strength from God to help you to forgive.

Scripture to Remember: "Do not repay anyone evil for evil. Be careful to do what is right in the eyes of everybody. If it is possible, as far as it depends on you, live at peace with everyone. Do not take revenge, my friends, but leave room for God's wrath, for it is written: 'It is mine to avenge: I will repay,' says the Lord. On the contrary: 'If your enemy is hungry, feed him; if he is thirsty, give him something to drink. In doing this, you will heap burning coals on his head.' Do not be overcome by evil, but overcome evil with good." (Romans 12:17–21 NIV)

Grief: I Can't Move Forward
After This Loss

 "We don't 'move on' from grief. We move forward with it."

-Nora McInerny

L auren was a preacher's kid who grew up in the church and loved the Lord. She and her younger sister Kristen were only 20 months apart in age and had a uniquely close sister bond.

Once Lauren herself became a mother, the two sisters were rendered inseparable. With the new addition of a baby, Kristen was determined to earn the title of World's Best Aunt. Shortly after the birth of her niece, Kristen was diagnosed with congestive heart failure. She was forced to undergo medical treatments and surgery, but with her family by her side, the future looked bright. There was no doubt in Lauren's mind that Kristen would overcome this health scare and be the loving auntie that she was destined to be.

After the initial surgery, she was able to return home, and

she was doing well. However, the following year, things took a drastic turn for the worse. Kristen's health began to fail fast, and within a matter of days, she was gone. Her family was devastated beyond belief—especially Lauren. She began to question God. How could this happen? Kristen was 27 years old. Why did He allow her to die? Very quickly, her questioning turned into anger. She didn't stop believing in God, but she couldn't fix her mind to go to church and praise a God who took her sister away from her. Lauren just couldn't get beyond her grief.

Like so many people who have lost a loved one, Lauren was left with unanswered questions and a gaping hole in her heart. As much as we are aware that tomorrow is not promised, there is nothing that can completely prepare us for losing a person we love. Whether the death came without warning or was expected, grief has the ability to cast a dark shadow over our lives that can bring our world to a standstill. In these valley moments, it is easy for us to find ourselves stuck in the pain pit of grief. Although it is normal for us to experience feelings of depression after the loss of a loved one, we cannot stay there indefinitely.

The Stages of Grief

The Five Stages of Grief and Loss, written by Elisabeth Kübler-Ross in 1969, was first conducted to determine the grief process for someone who was terminally ill. The first stage she described was denial, where a person would struggle with confusion, avoidance of the issue, shock, or fear. Then she witnessed individuals going into the next phase, anger, where they would express frustrations, anxiety, and irritation toward those around them. The third phase of grief is bargaining, where an individual might try to make a deal with God, saying something to the effect of, "God, if you give me one last chance, I promise you I will do _____." This phase is followed by depression, where everything around a person feels numb or futile, and they have no desire to do anything that they used to love. Some people even find themselves questioning the point of life in this phase. The final phase Ross identified for terminally ill patients was acceptance. This phase doesn't mean you are happy about the situation, but it means that you have come to terms with the reality of your circumstances and are working toward understanding what it means for your life now.[1]

Following the completion of that study, it was determined that people go through the same stages of grief when they have experienced the loss of a loved one. She also confirmed from this study that everyone's grieving process is different. We can't assume a person's way of expressing anger will look the same as another's, or that they should be in a certain stage for a certain period of time, or even that they will hit the five stages in the same order as she suggested. Grief cannot fit inside a cookie-cutter framework. The only thing that is common ground for everyone when it comes to grief is that we will all experience it one day.

Grief is Something we Cannot Avoid

The reality of death can sometimes feel overwhelming. As a child and young adult, I always avoided having conversations about death. Whenever my father would try to talk to me about estate planning, I would immediately shut the uncomfortable conversation down. Similarly, if someone I knew experienced a death of a loved one, I would always struggle to find the right words to say to them.

I recall instances when I was so uncomfortable my anxiety would lead me to say something completely awkward to change the subject or I would blurt out the first Christian cliché that would come to my mind, such as "Time heals all wounds," or "At least they are in a better place." When in fact, time doesn't heal all wounds, and even if they are in heaven, it doesn't take away the fact that the person who is grieving would prefer to still have their loved one here with them. Seeing how none of my "well-intended" words ever seemed to help them, I started to avoid conversations with grieving people altogether. Instead of being at a place I could support them, those who were grieving would pick up on my uneasiness and would put on a mask of "strength" for me so I would be comfortable.

That response to grief is not uncommon. When it comes to death, many of us would prefer to glaze over the conversation. However, we have to learn to become comfortable with being uncomfortable. We must understand grief is an experience we will all have, so we must be willing to talk about it—especially if we are ever going to be able to help others. People we encounter in our day-to-day lives have lost children to tragic violence, have lost a spouse or parent to illness, have caught wind that their friends died in an unexpected accident. These moments can be life-shattering, but during these times we must be willing to be present with them in their pain. We must be able to let them know that they don't have to be strong, that it's okay to hurt because the pain they are experiencing shows they valued that person's life so much, their presence will be forever missed.

· · ·

Learning how to Move Forward

Nora McInerny, who hosts the "Terrible, Thanks for Asking" podcast on grief, understands the agony that it can bring upon a person all too well. In her 2018 Ted Talk, she described how she experienced three back-to-back deaths in a finite period of time. On October 3rd, Nora lost her second pregnancy; on October 8th, she lost her dad to cancer; and on November 25th, her husband Aaron died from brain cancer. Many people responded to her circumstance by saying, "I can't imagine." Her response to them was, "But I think you can, and I think you should because one day it's going to happen to you."[2]

Nora quickly recognized the importance of creating that space for people. In the midst of her grief, she created a support group called "The Hot Young Widow's Club," where her and other women could remove their mask and talk freely about their pain and their journey forward. Years later, Nora was blessed to fall in love again with a man she eventually married and started a new family with. However, even in the midst of her new marriage, she was very clear that Aaron (her first husband) would forever be a part of her second marriage. She recognized that she will always miss Aaron, but he helped her become the woman that she is today, and her family today is benefiting from the love he showed her. In the words of Nora, "We do not move on from the grief, we move forward with it."[3]

When we've experienced a major loss, it is wrong for us to adopt the misconception that someone can just "move on" from their grief. When should a parent who lost their child to gun violence "move on"? When do we "get over" the loss of a best friend, spouse, or parent? The answer is *never*. We cannot zap our brain and expect to not feel any more sadness from that loss. The pain we feel from grief is real and should not be minimized. We also must understand that the significance of our loss cannot be measured by a person's role in our lives—which is why we must avoid comparing our grief to someone else's. Creating that "new norm" after loss will be difficult, but it is only in "moving forward" that we are able to find our way out of the pain pit of grief.

I conducted an interview with Dr. Sunitha Chandy, a licensed clinical psychologist in the Chicagoland area, regarding her beliefs on the subject of pain, grief, and loss. Her understanding of the process of grief was so profound I felt it important to share:

"The grief process is something that we do to honor the value in life and hope for redemption...You create a place in your heart that is like soil...and in that soil, you have the opportunity to grow things in it. There are seasons where you see flowers bloom and you see beauty that has grown out of that hurt. Then there are winter seasons when it is just a place of pain. I think it is recognizing that the life that was lost is valuable...so we get to grieve, but we don't get to be consumed by it. That's what leads to destruction. That's when people turn to substance abuse, avoiding life, and ignoring the dirt by saying, 'I don't want to see it.' Then in contrast, you have the people who decide they want to control every-thing...and try to pave over this dirt. How can we get to the place where we ask, 'What do we do with this [dirt], because it's here and we don't get a choice to get rid of it? How can we respond and interact with it?' Your life can continue to grow beyond this, but the fact that this has happened to you will always be there. It's the idea that we are not going to erase it from your brain, but we do know how to help you build a life around it, so when you look at the story of your life, there is this stone that you wish you could remove in the midst of a forest of beauty."

This powerful illustration that Dr. Chandy painted serves as a reminder that it is not our goal to remove pain when we grieve. Rather, our goal should be to identify what steps we need to take to move forward *with* the pain. Moving forward looks different for everyone. For some it could be forming a support group; for others it might be volunteering with a cause that gives you meaning. For Lauren, who we met at the beginning of this chapter, her first steps toward moving forward began by slowly rebuilding her relationship with God. Lauren was invited one day to attend a monthly young adult gathering called CAYA, which stands for Come As You Are, hosted by Alfred Street Baptist Church in Alexandria, Virginia. This meeting gave her a sense of community among her peers, and after attending faithfully for four years, she eventually rejoined the church and recommitted herself to the Lord.

In doing so, God gave her a vision concerning how He was going to use her pain and struggle to help other people through their valleys of grief. Lauren turned her sister's death into a personal mission by working to prevent other people from dying of heart disease. She started an awareness campaign, #loveKris. To date, she has run seven half-marathons in memory of her sister, and she intends on running a total of 27 (one for each year of Kristin's life) to raise money for heart disease prevention. There is not a day that goes by where Lauren doesn't miss her sister, but she has made a decision to honor her sister by living her best life. Lauren hasn't "moved on," but she has definitely made a commitment to move forward. There are countless stories of people like Lauren out there in the world, and it is their light that they are able to shine in the midst of their pain, that gives the world hope.

Grieving a Lost Dream

I recently had the opportunity to visit Lauren's church to experience one of their CAYA events. Her pastor, Howard-John Wesley, happened to be teaching about the subject of grief and loss that day. I was struck by how transparent he was concerning his struggles with grief. Despite the difficulties of being vulnerable in front of so many people, Pastor Wesley shared his experience grieving the loss of his father, as well as grieving the loss of a marriage that ended in divorce. I am confident that his willingness to be candid and honest about the emotions he felt—especially speaking about the topic of divorce, which is judged harshly within the church—opened up the doors for other people to remove the mask they had been wearing to hide their shame and grief around that subject.

Pastor Wesley, like all of us, has experienced grief in ways beyond just the physical death of someone. If we go through a major breakup with someone we truly loved, we grieve. If our dream business we've invested our life savings into fails, we grieve. If we've desired with all our heart to give birth to a child, only to find out we are infertile, we grieve. When we see injustice, broken school systems, mass incarceration, and violence, we grieve. The death of any vision of an ideal future can cause us to grieve.

It is all the more challenging when we experience the loss of a dream we believed was given to us from God. In those cases, we are left with questions like, "God, did I really hear from you?" "Why did this happen?" "What could I have done to change this?" Pressing forward in the midst of these unanswered questions can be extremely difficult, but that is where our faith must be the driving force moving us forward.

We know that faith is the substance of things hoped for, the evidence of things not seen (Hebrews 11:1). Pressing forward in the midst of grief can be described in its simplest form as a faith walk. It is a belief that despite how bad I'm hurting right now, I will somehow make it through to brighter days. There will be days when we honestly feel as if we do not have the strength inside of us to move forward. As much as the pain from grief can be paralyzing, as believers, we cannot allow that grief to hold us captive. We must know that in spite of our loss, God still has work for us to do, and we cannot allow what happened to get in the way of that. Those are the times we as believers must pull from a strength that is greater than ourselves, knowing that God will sustain us even during our darkest moments.

The Poster Boy of Loss

If there could be a poster boy for loss in the Bible, I would nominate Job. Job went through a dark season where he was tested by God and lost his animals, his servants, all of his sons and daughters, and his health. His friends were asking what Job might have done to bring this loss upon himself, and his wife flat out told Job to "curse God and die" (Job 2:9). During this season, Job could have easily given up his faith, but instead he came before the feet of God with heartfelt laments:

"I cry out to you, God, but you do not answer; I stand up, but you merely look at me. You turn on me ruthlessly; with the might of your hand you attack me. You snatch me up and drive me before the wind; you toss me about in the storm. I know you will bring me down to death, to the place appointed for all the living. Surely no one lays a hand on a broken man when he cries for help in his distress. Have I not wept for those in trouble? Has not my soul grieved for the poor? Yet when I hoped for good, evil came; when I looked for light, then came darkness. The churning inside me never stops; days of suffering confront me" (Job 30:20–27).

From Job's lament, we see how he chose to run *to* God, not *from* God. Job was not afraid to bring his pain to God and ask tough questions as to why He would allow this to happen. As children of God, we have the right to ask Him questions in our pain. We might not always get an answer, but God is always present with us in our loss. The Lord is close to the brokenhearted. He saves those whose spirits have been crushed (Psalm 34:18 NRSV).

God wants to be there to comfort us, but we must make the first step. Let us always remember that we can bring our pain to God, allowing Him to wrap His arms around us and hold us up during our time of grief. Let us find our strength in Him to keep moving forward.

Chapter 5 Reflection

Key Point: Grief is not an experience to be avoided. We all will experience it, and when we do, let us run *to* God for comfort, versus running *from* Him.

Questions to Consider: Have you experienced a loss that has caused you to feel stuck in the pain pit of grief? If so, what is one small step you can take to move forward in the midst of your pain?

Scripture to Remember: "Blessed are those who mourn, for they will be comforted." (Matthew 5:4 NIV)

Where Pain Meets the Mask

 "Sometimes the biggest smiles hide the most pain."

-Unknown

I avoided the doctor for years. In my mind, if I exercised regularly, maintained a good diet, and was in overall good health, there was no need to go. That changed for me last year, when I decided to participate in a free wellness check offered by my job. When the nurse explained the results to me, she said that everything looked good, but this wellness check was not a substitute for me going to the actual doctor. Then, in a cavalier tone, she said, "People tend to only go to the doctor when there's an emergency, but the emergency could have potentially been avoided if they were proactive about their health."

After I left the appointment, I took a moment to reflect on what the nurse said. She was right. I began to think about how we will do everything in our power to avoid going to the doctor's office by taking a bunch of over-the-counter medications, experimenting with grandma's hot toddy recipes, and trying some other concoctions that we've researched online. Although those methods might relieve the symptoms, they never help us to identify the cause of the problem. With our limited knowledge and resources, we might assume the symptoms are the result of one thing, when in all reality, it reflects a different, deeper issue that only a doctor can properly diagnose.

Just as we try to fix our physical health issues on our own, we are quick to do the same with emotional pain. Instead of going to God—the doctor who is able to diagnose and guide us along the path to healing—we search elsewhere for generic, convenient solutions to make us feel better but never address the root cause of our pain. This form of "treatment" or "self-medicating" masks the pain, but does not heal it.

While we may take an aspirin to ease the pain of a broken arm, we wouldn't expect it to actually heal the injury. For that, we would need to see a medical professional. The same applies to our spiritual life. Often, it takes an absolute state of emergency to get us to realize we need God. However, by the time we figure that out, a lot of damage has already been done.

Through my ministry work at Faith on the Journey (which tells testimonies of believers to help grow their faith), I've heard countless stories from people who went down a path of self-destruction as a result of abuse, trauma, or other pain they experienced in their past. Their pain was so overwhelming they either attempted to "numb" the pain or they fought to get "power and control" over it.

. . .

Numbing our Pain Behind the Mask

It is a common misconception that the only people who numb their pain are alcoholics or are addicted to drugs. There are many ways people numb (or mask) their pain that are considered socially acceptable. Think about it. Have you ever poured yourself into work or ministry to stop thinking about a painful event in your past? Have you ever jumped into a rebound relationship to forget about a break-up? Shoot, have you ever found yourself sitting in front of the television eating a tub of ice cream just to take your mind off a Monday from hell? Both my hands are raised for that one!

The truth of the matter is, we've all chosen to numb ourselves at some point rather than deal with harsh realities. We have to understand that if we consistently turn to anything for relief in lieu of facing the issue at hand, we have allowed our escape to become an addiction. Brené Brown, PhD, who is a professor and a licensed clinical social worker, said, "Addiction can be described as chronically and compulsively numbing and taking the edge off of feelings."[1] Simply put, anything that we do, even if it is considered a "good" thing, can become an addiction if we are not careful. Food can become an addiction. Shopping can become an addiction. Social media can become an addiction. I've learned from first-hand experience that work can become an addiction, too.

I've been referred to as a "workaholic" for the majority of my adult life. For years, I embraced that title like a badge of honor. However, as I got older, I realized I was using work and ministry as an escape so I didn't have to deal with deeper issues beneath the surface, such as my struggles with self-esteem and shame. This fast-paced life got in the way of spending time with family and close friends, and being present in romantic relationships. Being labeled a workaholic wasn't a good thing. It didn't help me resolve underlying issues, and other areas of my life suffered in the process.

That's the problem with choosing to numb pain. Although it offers short-term relief, the feelings that are covered up are still there. When we mask pain, we have to resort back to that same "escape" or addiction over and over again—usually in a higher dosage—just to get some relief. That temporary solution will never be enough to completely take away the hurt we feel inside. Even if we have mastered the art of hiding behind the mask, the undealt-with emotions will one day rise to the surface.

The second major problem with this path is that we are unable to pick and choose which emotions we turn off. Brené Brown conducted extensive research concerning people who choose to mask their pain. In her studies, she found there is no such thing as selective emotional numbing. In other words, when we choose to numb the dark things in our lives, we also numb the light.[2] In doing so, we are missing the opportunity to experience the fullness of everything that God wants to offer us, like feelings of love, peace, and joy.

The former 1958 Miss America knows this to be true. Marilyn Van Derbur describes her full story in her book, *Miss America By Day*. She was a victim of incestual rape. Her father molested her from the age of 5 to 18. She recalls feeling as if there was no escape from the abuse. Her father was wealthy and held in high esteem throughout the community, and her family was able to maintain the image of a picture-perfect family throughout her childhood and her early adult years. Her sisters also experienced abuse at the hands of their father. Everyone in the family had mastered the art of wearing the mask.

Marilyn went on to find great success following her abuse.

She graduated with honors from college, was named the Outstanding Woman Speaker, and received a host of other accolades. Life was good, and it seemed like she had learned to mask her pain with success. She made a decision to never revisit what happened to her as a child, but the pain from that abuse continued to fester under the surface. She began self-sabotaging her relationship with the man she loved, she made impulsive decisions, and was an emotional wreck. One day, at the age of 39, everything in her life came to a screeching halt. She went into physical paralysis. Her mind was working, but her body wouldn't move. The doctors said they couldn't find anything wrong with her, but the symptoms continued on and off for 11 years.

During therapy, she realized she lived a life of isolation. Although she knew how to wear her mask well, she never had any real connections with people. Why? Because Marilyn always felt she could never allow herself to be known, believing "if you knew this about me, you would never want to speak to me again."[3] It wasn't until she finally removed the mask and began to go to therapy to deal with her pain that she was able to begin the healing process. Although it took several years to begin her journey toward healing, she felt freedom from the shackles of her past once she made the decision to confront the pain that had imprisoned her versus running from it.

The longer you run from your pain, the longer it has the ability to control you. You might not think it at the time—you actually might believe you have control over the situation, like someone driving under the influence. However, the influence that unresolved pain can have over your life is deeper than you can imagine. It can not only cause you to veer off the path that you are supposed to be on, but can also result in a lot of casualties—including your own—if left unaddressed.

Wearing the Mask of Power and Control

Power and control are other ways in which we work to cover up the pain inside. We can go to extreme lengths to prevent others from seeing the wounds beneath our mask, especially when we are struggling with a sense of shame. These defense mechanisms (or masks) we choose are our strategy for survival, aiming to protect ourselves from further exposure to shame.

Robert Albers, PhD, who served as a professor of pastoral theology and ministry at Luther Seminary in St. Paul, Minnesota, wrote an excellent book on shame, entitled *Shame: A Faith Perspective*.[4] In his book, he identified several defense mechanisms (or masks) that people use to avoid rekindling that feeling. I firmly believe that several of the masks that he identified are also used by people who are wrestling with unforgiveness and feelings of loss. Let's explore some of these masks together.

Perfectionism Mask

When we fall short of an idealized image, it results in us feeling disgusted by ourselves. We believe one way to avoid shame is to live a perfect life, thereby eliminating any chances of being criticized or attacked. This defense mechanism, which is often birthed from an individual having unreasonable expectations from their parents at an early age, causes us to strive for a divine attribute that is impossible for human attainment. Later in life, however, it is no longer the parents or an external party making these demands, but us making the demands of perfection upon ourselves. A viciously competitive mindset can be a byproduct of this, where we develop a motto of "winning is not everything—it's the only thing!" When we lose or fall behind, envy is quick to raise its head. From a biblical standpoint, we can mistakenly believe we are mandated by scriptures to be perfect and are driven toward perfection in order to earn God's acceptance.

Self-Righteous or Scapegoating Mask

The self-righteous mask is easily identified as those of us who act as if we are "holier than thou." With this mask, it is easier to project shame onto others than to deal with our own shame. We have a tendency to be judgmental, fault-finding, or condescending toward others. This gives us a feeling of control. We have a need to feel good about ourselves, which we have learned to accomplish by either putting others down or putting ourselves forward.

Similar to the self-righteous mask, some of us prefer to wear the scapegoating mask. This is a popular defense mechanism where we not only like to find fault in others, but we blame others for our own problems. Those of us who wear this mask often respond with statements such as, "This wouldn't have happened if it weren't for you," casting shame onto others. Many times we will often choose to take out our pain on the ones that are closest to us. We see this represented in abusive relationships, where an individual would rather transfer their pain onto someone else than to confront their own vulnerabilities.

. . .

Martyr or Loner Mask

These two masks are especially prevalent throughout the church. Those of us who wear the martyr mask like to assume the role of the one who is the servant of all servants. This indirectly serves as a way to edify ourselves. Under these masks, there is no real giving of ourselves for the sake of others—instead, we are motivated to protect ourselves against being shamed or hurt by others by "self-shaming" or being the "sacrificial lamb." For those of us who are loners, we live by the mantra of, "If they can't get to me, they can't hurt me." We strive to create a safe world in which there is no room for additional hurt, because there is no room for anyone else to get in. Those of us wearing this mask often struggle with intimacy in relationships and expressing emotions.

Understanding our Emotions:

As we journey toward uncovering the emotions behind the mask, it's important that we take a moment to define what emotions are. According to Oxford Dictionary, emotions are "strong feelings deriving from one's circumstances, mood, or relationships with others."[5] The emotions we feel are identified as either primary or secondary emotions. Primary emotions can be described as the emotions that individuals feel first regarding a situation. For example, if someone loses a loved one, their primary emotional response might be sadness. Secondary emotions are feelings that arise after the primary emotions. In that same example, after the person has moved beyond their initial response of sadness, they might become angry. It's important to note that in certain instances a primary emotion in one scenario (i.e., anger) can serve as a secondary emotion in another.[6]

This theory is important to understand when we are trying to gain an understanding of what is happening with us behind the mask. When we look at what caused the devastating sinking of the Titanic in 1912, it wasn't the tip of the iceberg that caused the ship to sink—it was the massiveness of the iceberg underneath the water that brought the ship to its demise. The same truth applies to us. In most cases, the emotions other people see on the surface are usually just the tip of the iceberg. The unconscious emotions that lie underneath drive our behavior. They have the power to destroy us. It is critically important to deal with pain from our past so we don't end up hurting ourselves or others. The anger iceberg illustration is the perfect example of this.

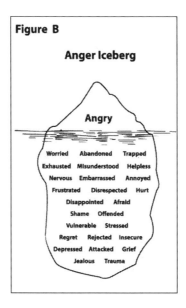

Figure B describes anger as an iceberg, where a particular emotion is visible above the surface, but other emotions exist below the waterline that are not initially obvious to the naked eye. In these cases, the secondary emotion of anger is projected to protect us from having to reveal to others vulnerable feelings that lie beneath the surface. Depending on the circumstances, we might have felt offended, trapped, disrespected, and so on. The emotions hidden under the iceberg can become evident to people we interact with, but the reason why we are behaving that way could be hard to pinpoint. For example, you might know someone who always seems to be angry, aggressive, controlling, and mean-spirited. This emotion (or mask) of anger that they project is just the tip of the iceberg, reflecting unresolved emotions of offense, hurt, or shame underneath the surface.[7]

I must warn you that dealing with pain from your past will not be easy. In fact, it will probably be one of the most difficult things you have done in your life. However, in order to enjoy the life that God wants to give you, you must confront your pain. You have no other choice.

Chapter 6 Reflection

Key Point: When we see individuals act in offensive or destructive ways, it is a reflection of deeper issues that lie beneath the surface.

Questions to Consider: Are there ways you have chosen to either numb or gain power and control over your pain? If so, how?

Scripture to Remember: "Fear not, for I am with you; be not dismayed, for I am your God; I will strengthen you, I will help you, I will uphold you with my righteous right hand." (Isaiah 41:10 ESV)

Finding the Courage to Remove the Mask

 "In a world where everyone wears a mask, it is a privilege to see a soul."

-Unknown

I never knew the power that the mask had over me until a facilitator asked a single question at a women's retreat: "Can you share with the group one experience you have gone through in life that broke you?"

When she first asked the question, I had no intentions whatsoever to share my business. I didn't know those people like that! Then, one very painful moment from a previous relationship came to mind. My heart began to race as it got closer to my time to share. I began to have a dialogue back and forth with God, saying, "God, I know you are not going to make me embarrass myself in front of all of these people." I did not want to remove my mask. I was so afraid that people in the room would look at me differently. Finally, just before the facilitator got to me, God convinced me that I needed to share my story with those in the room.

The facilitator gestured for me to speak. When I finally mustered up enough courage to open my mouth, water was welling up in my tear ducts and I could barely breathe. As I gasped for air, the words that described the past trauma began to form. I shared a story in that room that day that only a few people had ever known. After I finally finished speaking, I caught my breath, wiped my tears, and prayed silently. I couldn't believe I shared what happened to me. The mask I had worn for so long was no longer there to protect me. The devil quickly tried to attack my mind with feelings of shame, but God responded immediately in a way that I would have never expected.

As soon as the session was over, three different women who I never met before came up to me and said that they had gone through the same experience, too, but were too ashamed to share. I was floored. They told me that the courage I had to speak about my experience and remove my mask helped them realize that they were not alone in their struggle toward healing. God taught me a very valuable lesson that day. He showed me that when a single person makes the first step to remove their mask, it gives other people the courage to break free from their masks as well.

After my experience at the retreat, God gave me the revelation that people we know from work, church, or even our intramural basketball team could be struggling with the exact same issues as us. However, the enemy does his best to make us feel like we are alone in our struggles. He is lying. The Bible says, "What has been will be again, what has been done will be done again; there is nothing new under the sun" (Ecclesiastes 1:9). There is nothing in this world that we are confronted with that someone hasn't gone through before. Celebrities, faith leaders, our neighbors who look like they have the dream family, *everybody* has these struggles. Our challenge is that we are all scared to be judged, so we don't talk about the pain behind the mask.

Wearing a Mask Around Those we Love

I've come across situations in ministry where individuals who were married held painful secrets from their spouses—secrets of being sexually or physically abused as a child, STDs, criminal history, and past abortions, just to name a few. These are major events that can significantly impact how we see the world. Harboring secrets of this nature also has the ability to negatively affect intimacy and communication within a marriage. Withholding this information takes away a spouse's opportunity to prove that their love for us is not swayed by the painful events of our past. Our significant other wants to see who we genuinely are without the mask so they can truly understand and support us on our path toward healing.

We see a similar interaction between parents and their children. It is not uncommon for parents who have been abused as children to refuse to ever talk about what happened to them when they were growing up. When their child experiences the same type of trauma as the parent, the child is left thinking no one understands and there is no one they can talk to. The child keeps their trauma a secret, too, causing the cycle to continue.

Generational masks are passed down among these families. We have to learn to take the mask down in front of those people we love. We can't experience the depths of someone's love for us if we aren't willing to allow them to see the good, the bad, and ugly parts of what makes us who we are. If you have been wearing a mask to hide a secret that has been holding you captive, I am talking to you right now. You *must* find the courage to remove your mask, and the best place to start is with someone who you know and trust.

Brené Brown, a research professor at the University of Houston who's spent the last two decades studying vulnerability, shame, and empathy, once said, "We have to own our story and share it with someone who has earned the right to hear it, someone whom we can count on to respond with compassion."[1] This is not limited to a spouse or parent. You can choose to confide in a dear friend, a trusted advisor, or a pastor. The choice is yours, but at the end of the day, you must begin somewhere. It will feel unbelievably scary at first, but I promise you, it will be worth it.

Embarking on the Path to Freedom

Following my experience sharing my story at the retreat, I felt a sense of freedom, like handcuffs that had been tightly clamped around my wrists were finally cut off. When you allow people to see you without your mask, even for a moment, it takes away a bit of control your past had over you. If removed in a safe space, it also proves there are people who see you for who you are and love you and support you without judgement.

Removing the mask requires courage and a level of vulnerability that is in direct opposition to what the mask represents. This requires us to change the meaning we assign to the word "vulnerability" from a sign of weakness to a position of strength.

It is only when we make a decision to bring our hidden stories to light and start to deconstruct the narrative that we have believed about the pain of our past that we will begin to embark on our journey toward healing. I'm a firm believer in the old saying, "We are not defined by our circumstances. We are defined by how we choose to respond to our circumstances."

A friend of mine named Nicole Caley taught me this valuable lesson. Nicole has faced a number of major challenges in life, including overcoming abuse, neglect, and the loss of several close friends as a child. She could have easily allowed her pain to serve as an excuse for her to self-destruct. Although the pain from her past had a hold over her life for several years, Nicole eventually discovered she had the power to choose something different. In an interview I held with Nicole, she shared:

> "Sometimes the first part of this [process] is making the choice to say, 'I have to do this... because *the only way to heal is to hurt.*'"

Nicole's healing process was brutally painful, but she chose to keep pushing forward because she knew God had more in store for her life. Nicole understood the role pain plays in our lives. Pain is a part of the human experience. We can choose to deal with the pain now and allow God to work on healing the broken wounds of our heart, or we can try to avoid the pain and continue to walk with an emotional limp.

Romal Tune, a son of a drug-addicted mother, shared his story of healing in his book *Love is an Inside Job*. He recalled how he broke his ankle when he was a kid playing football.

His doctor told him that his ankle could be healed without him resetting it, but he would always walk with a limp. However, if he chose to have his ankle reset, which would require doctors to break his ankle again and align it, he would never have the problem again. The first option was the easiest option at the time, but the second, more painful option allowed him to experience full physical healing later on in life.

While Romal was going through therapy later in life, he realized this could be applied as a metaphor to all pain. If he made the choice not to deal with his emotional pain from the past by masking it, he would have continued the rest of his life walking with an "emotional limp." However, by going through the "re-breaking" process of confronting his pain and reliving those moments from his past, he was able to effectively begin his healing process that realigned everything. Eventually, after the rehabilitation process, he would be healed the right way. [2]

God wants to completely heal us and wants us to know that our story does not have to end at the source of our pain. Yes, there have been some painful chapters in our lives, but the book is still being written. We must have faith the ending will not be dictated by the pain of our past. Let us have courage knowing God is standing right with us as we embark on this journey. The Word of God says, "So do not fear, for I am with you; do not be dismayed, for I am your God. I will strengthen you and help you; I will uphold you with my righteous right hand" (Isaiah 41:10). He is our strength, and He will see us through to the end.

Chapter 7 Reflection

Key Point: In order to heal, we must be willing to experience pain.

Question to Consider: Are there people in your life who you consider a part of your inner circle (i.e., spouse, children, parents, close friends) who you still wear a mask around?

Scripture to Remember: "Therefore we do not lose heart. Though outwardly we are wasting away, yet inwardly we are being renewed day by day. For our light and momentary troubles are achieving for us an eternal glory that far outweighs them all. So we fix our eyes not on what is seen, but on what is unseen, since what is seen is temporary, but what is unseen is eternal." (2 Corinthians 4:16–18 NIV)

8

Healing Beyond the Mask

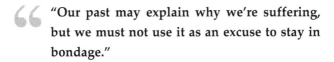 **"Our past may explain why we're suffering, but we must not use it as an excuse to stay in bondage."**

-Joyce Meyer, Battlefield of the Mind

The Bible is a book full of wisdom, adventurous stories, and the greatest love story ever told—that of a crucified Christ who loved us so much that He died for you and me. Jesus Christ, who walked the earth for only 33 years, performed 37 recorded miracles during his three active years of ministry. Of those miracles recorded, He performed 28 healing miracles. It is evident from Christ's ministry that God places the utmost importance on healing.

The Bible says, "For I will restore health unto thee, and I will heal thee of thy wounds, saith the Lord" (Jeremiah 30:17). This promise is not just for our physical healing, but also applies to the healing of broken places in our soul. However, it's important to recognize when we read about the healing miracles Jesus performed that everyone's healing experiences were different. The amount of time someone was sick before being healed was not the same. Their journey to find Jesus to receive healing was unique. The method, location, and the amount of time it took for Jesus to heal people all varied. Jesus healed Peter's feverish mother-in-law by merely touching her hand (Matthew 8:14–15). Jesus healed a blind man by spitting in the dirt, rubbing the mud on the man's eyes, and then instructing him to wash his face in the pool of Siloam (John 9:1–12). The process of healing was different, but the outcome was the same: God's children walked away healed.

Just like each person's healing experience was different in the Bible, each of our healing journeys will be uniquely designed for our needs as well. I continue to use the word *journey* through this book because this process requires time and effort. Although God has the ability to heal us instantaneously, oftentimes he wants us to be actively involved in the process to build our faith. The Bible shares with us several stories of individuals who had to overcome major obstacles to experience their healing.

Prior to coming to Jesus, the woman with the blood issue was sick for 12 years. She went to every doctor she could find, and they were unable to help her. She could have easily given up then, but she kept fighting for healing. When she heard about Jesus, she pressed her way through the crowd to get to him, and just by touching the hem of His garment, she was healed (Luke 8:43–48)! Another example is the paralyzed man who had his friends bring him to Jesus. He was so determined to get to Jesus he had his friends carry him on top of the roof, and make a hole in it so he could be lowered down to Jesus. That man walked away healed (Mark 2:1–12).

They were in need of healing, and they were willing to do whatever it took to get it. We have to be so determined to experience emotional healing from God that we are willing to do whatever it takes.

Although there is no magical "one size fits all" formula to find emotional healing, I will spend the rest of this chapter sharing six areas of focus that I would like you to explore. Under the guidance of the Holy Spirit, seek to identify how these areas of focus can be tailored to your specific needs so it can have the biggest impact. In other words, I want you to think about incorporating into your healing process whatever S.E.R.V.E.S. you the best. S.E.R.V.E.S. is an acronym that stands for Spirituality, Expression, Renewing of Mind, Vision, Embrace Life, and Support System. Let us begin.

Spirituality

When it comes to emotional healing, our faith must serve as the centerpiece of it all. Time and time again in the Bible, Jesus asked those he healed, "Do you believe?" and responded after their healing that "Your faith has healed you." It is our understanding that healing is a promise from God that will give us the strength to confront the pain from our path and embrace the gifts that God has in store for us.

It is equally important for us to understand the type of fight we are in. The Bible says, "Our struggle is not against flesh and blood, but against the rulers, against the authorities, against the powers of this dark world and against the spiritual forces of evil in the heavenly realms" (Ephesians 6:12 NIV). We are in spiritual warfare, and the adversary (Satan) plans to do everything in his power to keep us submissive to his will by keeping us enslaved by the pain of our past. If you attempt to fight a spiritual war with fleshly tactics, you will lose every time. Our battle requires spiritual warfare, which involves more than just a cutesy prayer. It means travailing before God in our petitions to Him.

Travailing is defined in the dictionary as engaging in a painful or laborious effort. When it comes to spiritual warfare, we are using every piece of energy we have to fight for the healing that is ours. I imagine blind Bartimaeus doing just that. When he heard Jesus was passing by, he did everything in his power to get His attention. Despite the objections of the disciples, he kept screaming at the top of his lungs, "JESUS! Son of David, have mercy on me!" (Mark 10: 48). Bartimaeus received his healing from Jesus that day, but I believe if he was passive and gave up after shouting Jesus's name once, there would have been a different outcome.

Like Bartimaeus, we cannot be passive or timid when it comes to our healing. We have to be intentional with our prayers, speaking God's words back to Him boldly in faith, thereby destroying any bonds that Satan has on us. When we do this, the power that is rightfully ours as children of God is released, and our Lord is able to begin the process of healing the broken places of our soul.

Express

When we have hidden our pain behind the mask for so many years, it is important that we identify safe outlets to express our pain.

Express Through Writing

There is something about the written word that is therapeutic to an individual who is working through the pain of their past. In a report produced by the Department of Family Medicine and Community Health, the University of Wisconsin, and the Pacific Institute for Research and Evaluation, they found that "the simple act of expressing thoughts and feelings on paper about challenging and upsetting events can allow us to move forward by expressing and letting go of the feelings involved. Expressive writing also provides an opportunity to construct a meaningful personal narrative about what happened. It brings clarity and enables us to place our experience into the context of our larger place in this world." [1] I've journaled on and off since my early 20s, and it has been a surreal experience to read through my old journals and see not only my thought process from years ago, but how God has brought me so far along in my journey.

Express Through Action

Sometimes words are not enough to express the pain that we are harboring in our hearts. In those cases, one must leverage their pain as the fuel for meaningful action. In Chicago, gun violence is an all-too-common tragic event. Year after year, we hear stories of individuals losing their lives at the hands of someone holding a gun. During my time working at St. Sabina Church in Chicago, I have frequently interacted with members of a group entitled Purpose Over Pain. This organization was started by parents who tragically lost their children to gun violence. These parents decided to channel their pain into something positive by developing a support group for other parents and family members who have lost a loved one to gun violence.

They work together to create a better and safer community by offering programs for children, resources for the community, and advocating for changes in laws on a local, state, and national level. Although there is nothing that can be done to bring their children back to them, the memory of their children lives on through the selfless work they do in the community to give other children a chance to grow up and live a meaningful life. Like Purpose Over Pain, one way you can choose to express your pain is through action. Consider volunteering. In some cases, you might be led to start your own nonprofit, mentoring program, or support group. Whatever we choose to do, engaging in action with a purpose can move us one step closer to our healing.

Another way to take action is through creative expression. Some of the most powerful songs ever written were by people lamenting about pain. If music is not your gift, quite possibly there is another creative outlet—like dance, art, poetry, or film—that you can use to express the creative ideas inside of you. Honing in on the creative gifts God gave you can serve as a healthy outlet and can inspire others along the way as well.

Express by Sharing Your Story

Sharing our stories in a safe environment, where we are surrounded by individuals who love and support us, can play a key role in the healing process. I recommend first sharing with a close friend, spouse, family member, or counselor. The first time sharing can be pretty scary, but if done with the right person, it can serve as a big step forward for us. For those of us who are further along in our healing journey, we might feel comfortable sharing our testimony with people more openly, like at church, conferences, workshops, etc. We will discuss the importance of using discernment when sharing in the next chapter.

Express Your Pain to a Counselor

We all need someone to talk to about our inner struggles, but sometimes we fear burdening our friends and family with our problems. What has helped me is going to see a counselor. Unfortunately, there has been a stigma placed on seeing a therapist due to the false belief that someone is "crazy" or something is "wrong" with them if they go to counseling. Seeing a therapist doesn't mean we're "crazy." It just means that we value our emotional health and are willing to take the necessary steps to be our best. A therapist has the ability to listen to us in a non-judgmental way and help us connect the dots to patterns and behaviors that might have otherwise been overlooked. If we have kept pain bottled up for years, it is crucial for us to have someone who can help deconstruct some toxic beliefs we have adopted and assign new meaning so we can begin to move forward in freedom.

Renewing Your Mind

Renewing your mind is a crucial step in your path toward healing, but probably one of the most difficult steps to do. The Bible speaks at length about the importance of renewing your mind. Romans 12:2 says, "Do not conform to the pattern of this world, but *be transformed by the renewing of your mind.* Then you will be able to test and approve what God's will is —his good, pleasing and perfect will." As believers, one major step that we must take is studying and meditating on God's word. This enables us to discern the truth of what God says about our situation in response to Satan's lies. The only way to combat lies is with truth. Knowing God's word in your heart will position you to win the battle in your mind.

We also must remember that our subconscious mind is hardwired to work a certain way and is shaped by the familiar past. However, modern science has proven that our minds can be rewired through neuroplasticity. In other words, although our brains have been wired to think a certain way for years, if we are intentional about changing the patterns of the brain, we will be able to change the way we think. [2]

One way to do this is to recite daily affirmations. Affirmations can help renew our minds by replacing self-sabotaging thoughts with beliefs that give life and peace. Spiritual affirmations are even more powerful because they are grounded in the word of God. Instead of saying you are a victim, begin to use language like, "I am a survivor." Instead of calling yourself a failure, call yourself an *overcomer*. As you begin to change the narrative you tell yourself, it will eventually change the perspective in which you view the pain from your past and life in general.

Vision

It always amazes me to see how easy it is for children to dream. If you ask them what they want to be when they grow up, they might spit off ten different answers. The sky's the limit for them, but for us it's not that simple. Many of us have stopped dreaming due to past failures, overwhelming lives, or negative experiences that have clouded our vision. The good news is that can all change today. I'm going to ask you to do one important exercise with me. Grab a piece of paper and a pen, right now.

Visualize yourself five years from now, but don't take into consideration your current or past circumstances. For just this moment, I want you to act as if your life's slate has been wiped clean and you have the chance to write your future for yourself. What would that look like? Where would you go? What gifts would you explore? Who would you work with? What initiatives would you start? What business or organization would you open? I don't care if you don't have the money for it, and I don't care if your situation looks nothing like that right now. For just one moment, *take the limits off!* Write down the first ten things that come to mind.

We often subconsciously limit ourselves by our past and current circumstances. With God, there are no limits. He wants to use us in ways we can't even imagine, but we have to be able to see beyond our "today" and "yesterday." That's why an exercise like this is so important. It helps to stretch our vision and gives us hope for the future. Now, if our vision for the future is rooted in desires of the flesh (i.e., lust, greed, selfish ambition), then God will not be a part of that. However, as we draw closer to God, our desires become more like His. The Bible says, "Take delight in the LORD, and He will give you the desires of your heart" (Psalms 37:4 NIV). If our desires are in line with God's, then we can be confident He is able and ready to open the floodgates for those of us who believe. Exercise your faith with me today, and begin to believe God for the greater things He wants to do through our lives.

Now let us say this prayer together:

"God, I'm sharing with you the desires of my heart today. Help me to not limit myself based on my past, but to remember that nothing is impossible with you. Please allow me to see myself the way you see me, and to fully explore the talents and gifts that you gave me on this earth so I can be used by you to help others embrace this life to the fullest. Amen."

Continue to make a commitment beyond today to pray over your list and add to it when other dreams come to mind. Then see how God will move in your life.

Embrace Life

Some people find it extremely difficult to embrace life after experiencing significant pain in their past. In those cases, a person might find themselves "existing" instead of "living." When we are merely existing, it hinders God from being able to fully use us.

Adopting a spirit of gratitude is one way in which we can learn to embrace life. A man named Hal Elrod was in a horrendous car accident in his early 20s. He arrived to the hospital unconscious, and when he woke up, he was told he had severe brain damage, 11 broken bones, and he would never walk again. His family was devastated by the news, but Hal had a different response. Hal looked at his situation from a place of gratitude, thanking God he was still alive. Hal made a decision that if he could never walk again, he was still going to choose to be happy and make the absolute most out of his life. However, he was going to exert all of his efforts into his healing, because despite what doctors said, he believed by faith that he would walk again. He visualized it, prayed about it, and focused all his attention on his goal to walk. Only a week later, Hal was able to take his first step. I wholeheartedly believe Hal received his healing because of his faith and spirit of gratitude. [3]

When we have a spirit of gratitude, we understand that

our worship is not determined by our circumstances, but rooted in something that doesn't change: the faithfulness of God.

The apostle Paul described this well when he said, "I know what it is to be in need, and I know what it is to have plenty. I have learned the secret of being content in any and every situation, whether well-fed or hungry, whether living in plenty or in want. I can do all this through Him who gives me strength" (Philippians 4:12–13).

We will go through rough patches in life we cannot control, but one thing we can control is our attitude. Let's choose to maintain a grateful heart and embrace life. If you've allowed yourself to get into a rut over the last several years, try to push yourself to have fun. Revisit an old passion you had for dancing or traveling, or try something new, like swimming with whales or skydiving. It might be as simple as spending more time with people you love. The possibilities are endless.

Support System

Developing a support system is absolutely essential in your journey forward. God did not create us to go through life alone, and we need people we can call on when we are struggling in our pain. I had a major setback in my healing process a few years ago. An issue from my past resurfaced, triggering a pain inside that nearly crippled me. I had important obligations that I needed to tend to at work, so I did my best to press through the pain. However, as I got in my car to head to work, I found myself crying uncontrollably. I could barely see the road through my tears. I realized in that moment that I needed to reach out to someone fast. I grabbed my phone and called one of my very close friends. When she answered, I could barely get two consecutive words out of my mouth. I finally calmed myself down enough to say three simple words, "I need you." Without hesitation, she said, "I will be at your house as soon as you get home." That made a world of difference, and though I still needed to work through some of my emotions after her visit, I felt like I had someone there to support me moving forward.

We all need real friends in our lives who we can call on at any time of day and whom we trust with the deepest secrets of our hearts. I encourage you to take a moment to think about the people in your life who are those friends to you. If you don't feel like you have any right now, my prayer is that God will bring those people into your life. In addition to receiving encouragement from your friends, support groups are another option to explore. They are designed to create a sense of community for you, and it allows you to meet with people who have gone through similar experiences as you. There are support groups for almost any issue, ranging from grief, addiction, abuse, etc. They will serve as a safe space for you to share your story.

The church is another key place we can turn to for support. The job of the church is to be a spiritual hospital for those who are hurting. Even though I realize that we can have a relationship with God outside of the church, when we don't go to church we lose the opportunity to befriend other Christians who can help us grow in our walk. For some of us, it is hard to consider going back to church because it has contributed to our pain. However, we cannot give someone who hurt us the power to control us for the rest of our lives. If you are in need of a church home, I encourage you to pray for

God to give you direction on what church is right for you, you can be a part of a community of believers.

I strongly believe if you pray about the ways you ca. incorporate this S.E.R.V.E.S. model into your life, God will begin to move in miraculous ways to allow you to experience the healing He has promised you.

Chapter 8 Reflection

Key Point: Everyone's journey to healing is different. However, anyone who experiences emotional healing must exercise their faith and be actively involved in the process.

Question to Consider: What are some practical steps you can incorporate from the S.E.R.V.E.S. model in your life today?

Scripture to Remember: "And the prayer of faith will save the one who is sick, and the Lord will raise him up. And if he has committed sins, he will be forgiven." (James 5:15 ESV)

Bonus resources for the S.E.R.V.E.S. model can be found at breakingthemask.com.

Showing Your Beauty Marks

 "Behind every scar is an untold story of survival."

-Rhys Wilkie

When I was a little girl, I was very self-conscious of three moles on my face. They seemed odd to me, especially since I noticed that other people didn't have them. It was only when I got older that I began to change the way I looked at them. Instead of referring to them as moles, I began to call them beauty marks. I noticed that they were placed on my face in a perfectly symmetrical angle, and it was a unique feature that I felt enhanced my beauty as opposed to taking from it.

I look at a person's testimony the same way. I see so much beauty in testimonies of individuals who have overcome great odds in life, especially when I witness how God brought a person out of their deepest pit to experience new life. Although we all love to hear a great comeback story, sometimes it's difficult to share our own—particularly when we are still wrestling with shame and guilt from our past.

The beauty of our testimony is based on what God was able to do in our life despite what we've done or what was done to us. Let's consider the story of the woman at the well (John 4:4–26). This Samaritan woman had a checkered past. She would go to the well at noon when no one else was there to avoid interacting with other people who might try to hold her background against her. When she encountered Jesus at the well, He immediately saw through the mask that she was wearing to hide her shame. Jesus told her everything she ever did in her past, but instead of judging her about it, He spoke truth to her in love. He directly spoke to the source of her shame, saying that she had five husbands and the man she was with now she wasn't married to.

An important misconception about this interaction is that this woman made a choice to have five different husbands, thereby making the assumption that she was promiscuous. A woman under the Pentateuch Jewish law would not have been allowed to choose to get a divorce. However, a man could issue a bill of divorce for any reason, ranging from a woman being barren to her looking at him the wrong way. We also know that the reason behind her multiple failed marriages wasn't due to her committing adultery, because we see later in this gospel that a woman committing adultery is punished by stoning (John 7:53–8:11). The only way she could have had five marriages is if the man divorced her or passed away. It is speculated by scholars that the sixth man she was living with refused to marry her.[1] Therefore, this woman's shame did not come from her being promiscuous, it came from the fact that she was dealing with feelings of loss and rejection from multiple men who told her she wasn't good enough.

Jesus taught her she didn't have to seek men to quench her desire to be wanted and valued. He was able to tell her about a living water, where she would never have to seek affirmation from man again but could receive the unconditional love she thirsted for from God. Her encounter with Jesus was so transformative that she went into town and shared with anyone she could what He did for her. I can only imagine when the people heard the conviction in her voice and saw her new level of confidence, they asked themselves, "Who is this 'Jesus'?" Many people committed their lives to Christ that day because she shared her story.

Like the woman at the well, many of us have had some negative experiences that have led other people to judge us. Yet, when God comes into our lives and transforms us, we are no longer held captive by the opinions of others because we understand that only our Creator can define who we are. It is in us experiencing this freedom that we can't help but tell others what God has done for us. We can't contain our praise because we remember how our lives used to be before Christ. The scars from our past are reminders of God's grace in our lives. In essence, our scars are beauty marks. You might say "beauty marks" is a bit of a stretch, and I recognize that this paradigm shift can be hard to embrace initially, but it's the only way I've been able to become accustomed to looking at someone's testimony.

What our Scars Represent

Although we might not look favorably upon a physical scar, a scar on our body reflects more than just the discolored skin we see with the naked eye. Our scars represent stories of painful experiences in our past that have significance. A scar could tell a story of surviving an accident that required years of rehab or the miracle of surviving a gunshot wound. Scars even represent the most significant story of our faith: the crucifixion of our savior Jesus Christ. Even after Jesus rose from the dead and appeared to his disciples in John 20:24–29, he still had his scars. The resurrected Christ could have easily removed any visible signs that reflected the horrific pain He endured on the cross, but He wanted His scars to serve as a reminder of the story of what He sacrificed for you and me.

Just as our physical scars have meaning, emotional scars we received from the pain and trauma of our past have significance, too. As much as a person might want the scar to go away, it will always be there, serving as a reminder of what happened. The good news is the scar doesn't only represent the pain that caused it, but tells the story of how God was able to resurrect us out of the dark places of our lives and set us on a new path. It shows the world that we were able to survive a painful experience, which gives those around us hope they can survive, too. It ultimately symbolizes God's healing in our lives, and when we understand that, there is no shame. Embracing this truth helps us to see that a scar is not something that should be frowned upon, but a beauty mark of God's grace.

We share our beauty marks with the world by telling our testimonies. A testimony, as defined from a faith perspective, is a public recounting of a religious conversion or experience. The sharing of one's testimony has been widely embraced as common practice in many churches today, where individuals will stand before the congregation and share the good news about what God has done in their lives. The sharing of a testimony in this setting can really help others to grow their faith, and God will use some of us in that fashion to help others find hope.

Discerning who we Share our Story With

Although I believe sharing our story is a critical part of our healing process, I've also learned that having discernment about when and how we tell our testimony is key. Beth Moore, a world-renowned evangelist, author, and Bible teacher, once said, "We must be authentic with all, transparent with most, but we can only be intimate with some." In some cases, God might lead us to only share parts of our story with the people in our inner circle, and that gives God glory, too.

Think about it. If we have a beauty mark located on an area of our body that is considered private (like your inner thigh or chest), it is not in a location designed to be shown to the entire world. Only people who share a very intimate space in our life will ever have the opportunity to see that. Likewise, sometimes God will say that this part of our testimony is only meant to be shared with those who are a part of an intimate space in our lives who we trust will honor the sacredness of our story.

In Professor Brené Brown's book, *The Gifts of Imperfections*, she warns us that "sharing our shame story with the wrong person can easily become a piece of flying debris in an already dangerous storm."[2] Gaining an understanding of to whom we can confide our deepest secrets can only be done by tapping into the wisdom that is available to us through the Holy Spirit. The Holy Spirit serves as a counselor and comforter throughout our entire journey in life (John 14:26

AMP). The counselor will nudge at our heart and give us guidance on when and how to share our story. As the Holy Spirit leads us to share our story, we will not only be provided with the courage we need to move forward but also receive the comfort of God's peace by knowing that He was with us in that moment.

Our Testimony is Meant to Help Someone Else

When I first started Faith on the Journey, I knew that creating a platform for people to hear various testimonies would be powerful. However, I never imagined how it would also help set free individuals who shared testimonies, because it allowed them an opportunity to come out from behind the mask. Several people I interviewed have never shared their testimonies before. Some individuals were still battling with shame and fear of what other people may think about their story, while others just didn't think their story mattered. By sharing their story openly through this platform, they began to realize the significance of why God allowed them to survive what they went through—to help someone else. I've come to recognize that our testimony doesn't belong to us. It belongs to God, and God wants to use our story to help someone else move forward along their journey.

Several years ago, I stopped by a local restaurant, and I ran into a young lady I knew named "Angel." I hadn't seen her in a few years, and I was so excited to catch up with her. I remembered her always being bubbly and full of energy, so when I saw her solemn demeanor I knew something was wrong. After engaging in small talk for a few moments, Angel began to share with me how difficult life had been for her recently. I could tell she was afraid of disappointing me, so she was apprehensive to share some of the details at first. I assured Angel that I would never judge her, and it was a safe space to share whatever was on her heart.

As she pressed through her tears to tell me her story, I became filled with compassion, as I saw the weight of the hurt and shame Angel carried on her shoulders. I understood the type of pain Angel was carrying because I had gone through some of the exact same experiences. God prompted me to share a part of my story with her so she could see that she wasn't alone. By hearing just a small part of my testimony, she immediately felt a glimpse of hope. She saw that someone who she looked up to had also gone down that road before. I continued to minister to Angel, reminding her that no matter how awful things are for her right now, God is still with her and He will see her through this valley in her life. Although I wasn't able to take Angel's pain away in that moment, I knew without a shadow of a doubt that God sent me there in that exact moment to serve as a light in the midst of Angel's darkness by sharing my story.

The Bible says, "They triumphed over him by the blood of the Lamb and by the word of their testimony" (Revelations 12:11). We overcome the enemy's tactics of isolation, condemnation, and shame by bringing our story to light and celebrating the power of God to restore us, even in the most broken places of our lives. If God is leading you to share your testimony, it is for a reason beyond yourself. God wants to use us to help free someone else who is struggling in silence. Our willingness to be vulnerable about our struggles will generate a feeling of connectedness with those who hear it, and will send them a message that if God was able to restore *us* from a dark place, God can absolutely restore them, too.

I want to encourage you to reflect on your testimony and

story of resilience. That's the part of your story that helped form you into the person you are today. Once you do that, I want you to say a short and simple prayer with me:

"God, I surrender my story to you. You are the ultimate author and editor of my story, and you have the right to use my testimony in any way you see fit to advance the kingdom. Please give me strength to share my story when you lead me to do so. I pray when I do share my story, others will draw closer to you and have a deeper understanding of your faithfulness, even in the midst of adversity. Amen."

Chapter 9 Reflection

Key Point: Behind every emotional scar, there is a story of survival and God's grace that sustained you during that difficult experience.

Question to Consider: What are some beauty marks that serve as a testimony of God's faithfulness in your life?

Scripture to Remember: "But Jesus said, 'No, go home to your family, and tell them everything the Lord has done for you and how merciful he has been.'" (Mark 5:19 NLT)

The Wounded Healer

 "Only the wounded healer can truly heal."

-Irvin D. Yalom

We have taken quite the journey together. We started the process of identifying various masks we've become accustomed to wearing in our day-to-day lives, we've taken an in-depth look at the three types of pain most often hidden behind the mask, and we've explored ways in which we can begin to experience healing in those areas of our lives.

If you've begun to do the work that has been outlined in this book and have been prayerful along the way, the healing in which you've been seeking is already well underway. You have been challenged to do uncomfortable things, but in doing so you have opened yourself up to more new things that God wants to do through you. As you continue on your journey toward healing, I'm going to give you one final challenge. I want you to bring someone with you along the way. God blesses us to be a blessing to others. If this book has blessed you in the way of healing, it is His will that you continue to share this good news with others.

While taking a class on pastoral care in seminary school, I was assigned to read *The Wounded Healer* by Henri J. M. Nouwen. The title of the book immediately intrigued me because of the dichotomous nature of the words "wound" and "heal." It's a paradox that begs the question: How can someone who is wounded, hurt, or broken be in a position to heal others? In my mind, it was akin to the blind leading the blind. However, God has radically changed that belief for me in recent years. God has shown me how he has chosen broken vessels to accomplish some of his greatest work.

We are God's Preferred Choice

Scripture tells us that "God chose the foolish things of the world to shame the wise; God chose the weak things of the world to shame the strong" (1 Corinthians 1:27). This is proof that God is not in the habit of using people who "have it all together" (as if anyone really does) to do His work. So many Christians have adopted the false belief that they cannot be fully used by God because of their brokenness. They are not "ready" to be used by God due to some areas of lack, pain, or sinfulness in their lives. These flaws we carry, hidden or pronounced, keep many of us distanced from stepping into the lives God is calling us to live. We have an "If I can just fix this area, God can use me" mindset.

This way of thinking is perpetually reinforced by our society. People are quick to judge and ostracize someone as a result of their previous mistakes or less-than-favorable circumstances. The good news is that the God we serve does not operate like that. When people choose to dismiss you because of your flaws, God says, "I want you in spite of your flaws." When people say you will never be able to get past a horrific moment in your life, God says, "I have a purpose and destiny for you that is greater than your past and what you could ever imagine for your future." Our Lord is searching far and wide for broken vessels who are willing to surrender themselves to Him, because in our brokenness, He is strong (2 Corinthians 12:9).

Examples of Wounded Healers

Just think about the countless examples in the Bible where God used broken people for some of his most important work. He used Noah, who was a drunk, to build the ark. He used Moses, who murdered someone and was a poor public speaker, to bring the Isrealites out of slavery and receive the Ten Commandments. He used Elijah, who was suicidal, as one of his greatest prophets. He chose David, who committed adultery and murder, to write a majority of the book of Psalms. He used Paul, who killed Christians for sport before his conversion, to write a majority of the New Testament and become one of his greatest evangelists.

God was not intimidated by their pasts, and neither is He with ours. He sees beyond our past. He sees beyond our "right now." He sees what He wants to do in us and through us. We can be confident that "He who began good work in you will carry it on to completion until the day of Christ Jesus" (Philippians 1:6 NIV). His work will forever continue in our lives until the day we leave this Earth. Until then, God calls us to serve Him as wounded healers.

Brenda Myers Powell, the co-founder of the Dream-Catcher Foundation, has answered the call to serve as a wounded healer. The first half of her life was engulfed in the world of drugs, sexual perversion, and violence. For over 25 years, she worked in all facets of prostitution. Brenda lost several of her friends to the streets and nearly lost her life after being shot and stabbed on multiple occasions.

One night, her dress got stuck in a customer's car door. She was dragged several blocks on the ground. The incident tore off pieces of her face and badly bruised the side of her body. When she went to the hospital, the staff in the emergency room laughed at her, treating her as if she was nothing but a whore that deserved what happened to her.

In that moment, Brenda decided she was no longer going to be a victim, and her journey toward healing began. As God continued to work on her heart, she began to gain a better sense of understanding of her value and her identity in Christ. It took God several years to heal Brenda from the trauma and shame from her past, but eventually God showed Brenda how he wanted to leverage her story of brokenness to save the lives of thousands of women today who have fallen into the world of prostitution. Through the DreamCatcher Foundation, Brenda and her team go out into the streets and minister to these women by showing them unconditional love and letting them know if they want to find a way out of prostitution, her team will walk that journey with them.

Brenda's life is the perfect personification of a wounded healer, but as much as God had a desire to use Brenda to do this work, He never would have forced her to do it. God will not force anyone's breakthrough, and He will not force you to be used. Brenda made the choice, and you have to make a choice, too. You can choose to limit how God uses you by looking at all of your shortcomings, mistakes, and barriers that confront you, or you can choose to surrender yourself—

even the ugly and broken parts of yourself—to be used by God to advance His agenda.

Live a Life of Freedom Beyond the Mask

God has allowed us to make it through our experiences for a reason. There have been countless individuals who have gone through similar circumstances as you who never made it to the other side of their mountain. They are either dead, have lost their minds, or are still held captive in that situation. He kept you, and it was for a purpose.

As you continue on your journey forward, ask God to reveal the ways in which He can use the pain from your past as a catalyst for something greater. The world needs you. Make a decision to answer God's call to be a wounded healer by helping others find freedom from the shackles of the mask. The light that shines through your life will let others know there is hope beyond the mask, there is joy beyond the mask, and there is healing for you and me beyond the mask.

Chapter 10 Reflection

Key Point: We don't have to have it "all together" for God to use us. God has used broken people for his greatest work.

Question to Consider: What is one way in which God can use you as a wounded healer?

Scripture to Remember: "But he said to me, 'My grace is sufficient for you, for my power is made perfect in weakness.' Therefore I will boast all the more gladly about my weaknesses, so that Christ's power may rest on me. That is why, for Christ's sake, I delight in weaknesses, in insults, in hardships, in persecutions, in difficulties. For when I am weak, then I am strong." (2 Corinthians 12:9–11 NIV)

11

Notes

Chapter 1

1. Carly Mallenbaum, Gaga shares mental health struggle, thoughts of suicide: 'My inner voice shut down' *USA TODAY*, November 9, 2018 https://www.usatoday.com/story/life/people/2018/11/09/lady-gaga-mental-health-patron-awards-sag/1940329002/

2. Sharon Waxman, "The Actor's Addiction" *The Washington Post*, November 28, 2000. https://www.washingtonpost.com/archive/lifestyle/2000/11/28/the-actors-addiction/54fb8326-1580-477d-a8d0-2edb8c11bd3b/?noredirect=on

3. Center for Disease Control and Prevention. "Drug Overdose Deaths." Last modified June 27, 2019. https://www.cdc.gov/drugoverdose/data/statedeaths.html

4. Center for Disease Control and Prevention. "During binges, U.S. adults have 17 billion drinks a year." Last modified on March 16, 2018. https://www.cdc.gov/media/releases/2018/p0316-binge-drinking.html

5. National Coalition Against Domestic Violence. "National Statistics Domestic Violence Fact" Sheet. Accessed July 18, 2019. https://www.speakcdn.com/assets/2497/domestic_violence2.pdf

6. Anxiety and Depression Association of America. "Understanding the Facts: Depression". Accessed July 28, 2019. https://adaa.org/understanding-anxiety/depression

7. Center for Disease Control and Prevention. "National Vital

Statistics Reports Volume 68, Number 9. Accessed August 20, 2019. https://www.cdc.gov/nchs/data/nvsr/nvsr68/nvsr68_09-508.pdf

Chapter 2

1. Dr. Joe Dispenza, "Unlock the Unlimited Power of Your Mind Today!" interview by Ed Mylett, March 21, 2019. https://www.youtube.com/watch?v=ereahWKwNV8.

Dr. Joe Dispenza "How to Unlock the Full Potential of Your Mind" interview by Tom Bilyeu, June 12, 2018. https://www.youtube.com/watch?v=La9oLLoI5Rc

2. Very Well Mind, "How the Fight or Flight Response Works," last modified August 18, 2019. https://www.verywellmind.com/what-is-the-fight-or-flight-response-2795194

3. Dr. Dispenza, interviews

Chapter 3:

1. Logos Bible Software 8.7.0.0042. Faithlife Corporation. www.logos.com. Guilt.

2. Logos Bible Software. 8.7.0.0042. Faithlife Corporation. www.logos.com. Conviction.

3. Albers, Robert. *Shame: A Faith Perspective* (New York: The Haworth Press, Inc., 1995), 25.

4. Albers, *Shame*, 25.

5. Brown, Brene. Listen to Shame, Ted Talk. March 16, 2012, Video, 14:08 https://www.youtube.com/watch?v=psN1DORYYV0&t=927s

Chapter 4:

1. Henning, Dave. 2012. "In the Shadow of the Cross" Crown of Compassion Ministries. February 11, 2019. https://www.crownofcompassion.org/2019/02/11/in-the-shadow-of-the-cross/

2. Ikari, Ben "African Cultural and Fundamental Rights Council Mourns and Celebrates Nelson Mandela," *Modern Ghana,* August 12, 2013, https://www.modernghana.com/news/507185/1/african-cultural-and-fundamenta.html

Chapter 5:

1. Gregory, Christina. "The Five Stages of Grief: An Examination of the Kubler-Ross Model" Psycom. Last Updated April 11, 2019. https://www.psycom.net/depression-medications/

2. McInerny, Nora "We Don't "Move on" from Grief. We Move Forward with It" Ted Talk , April 25, 2019. Video, 0:50 https://www.youtube.com/watch?v=khkJkR-ipfw

3. Mclnerny, *We Don't Move on from Grief.* 6:50

Chapter 6

1. Brown, Brene. *The Gifts of Imperfection*. (Hazelden Publishing: Minnesota, 2010), 70.

2. Brown, *The Gifts of Imperfection*, 72.

3. Van Derbur, Marilyn. "Marilyn Van Derbur. A Survivor Story" September 9, 2014. Video 5:42 https://youtu.be/YUDNs3cSOXU

4. Albers, Shame, 70-82.

5. Lexico, powered by Oxford. "Emotion" https://www.lexico.com/en/definition/emotion

6. Khan, Nadia "What Are Primary and Secondary Emotions," Better Help, last modified January 01, 2019. https://www.betterhelp.com/advice/general/what-are-primary-and-secondary-emotions/

7. Benson, Kyle, "The Anger Iceberg," The Gottman Institute, last modified November 8, 2016. https://www.gottman.com/blog/the-anger-iceberg/

Chapter 7

1. Brown, *The Gift of Imperfections*, 9.

2. Tune, Romal. *Love is an Inside Job: Getting Vulnerable with God*. (New York, Faith Words, 2018), 32-33.

Chapter 8:

1. VHA Office of Patient Centered Care and Cultural Transformation, "Whole Health: Change the Conversation: Advancing Skills in the Delivery of Personalized, Proactive, Patient-Driven Care" Accessed July 15, 2019: 1. http://projects.hsl.wisc.edu/SERVICE/modules/12/M12_CT_TherapeuticJournaling.pdf

2. Dr. Dispenza, interviews

3. Hal Elrod "If You Can't Change Your Emotions Do This Instead" interview by Tom Bilyeu, March 5, 2019. https://www.youtube.com/watch?v=g9yg5cDagJ0&t=313s

Chapter 9:

1. Meyer, Angela. "The Woman at the Well" Challenging Theology. December 8, 2014. https://medium.com/positive-theology/the-woman-at-the-well-the-radical-revelation-of-john-4-1-42-7aa3470f1b18

2. Brown, *The Gift of Imperfections*, 10.

STAY CONNECTED

SHARE YOUR THOUGHTS

Share your thoughts about this book with the
author, Jocelyn Jones, by emailing
info@breakingthemask.com.

Want to schedule a "Breaking the Power of the Mask" seminar
or retreat at your church or organization? Learn more by visiting
breakingthemask.com or emailing us at info@breakingthemask.com.

FREE ONLINE RESOURCES AVAILABLE AT

Breakingthemask.com.

Receive messages of strength, courage, and hope
by subscribing to our Faith on the Journey mailing list at
faithonthejourney.org.

If you have an amazing story to share of how God has delivered you
from a painful situation in your past, we want to hear from you.
Please contact us at info@faithonthejourney.org.

STAY INFORMED BY FOLLOWING US ON SOCIAL MEDIA

Like us on Facebook by visiting @faithonthejourney.
Follow Jocelyn Jones on Facebook @connectwithJocelyn
or on Instagram @myfaithonthejourney.